Paul Silvia's book of ad'                                    o
to know—and even mc
know—about how to get published in the best journals. And
he achieves all this with both wit and wisdom. This book is
essential reading for all graduate students and young faculty
pursuing careers in scientific research.

—**Dean Keith Simonton, PhD,** Distinguished Professor of
Psychology, University of California, Davis


Silvia does it again: *How to Write a Lot* inspired us to write,
and *Write It Up* provides the nuts and bolts on crafting a
high-impact—and even eloquent—empirical report.

—**John Dunlosky, PhD,** Department of Psychological Sciences,
Kent State University, Kent, Ohio

# Write It Up

## Practical Strategies for Writing and Publishing Journal Articles

Paul J. Silvia, PhD

AMERICAN PSYCHOLOGICAL ASSOCIATION • *Washington, DC*

Published by
APA LifeTools
American Psychological Association
750 First Street, NE
Washington, DC 20002
www.apa.org

To order
APA Order Department
P.O. Box 92984
Washington, DC 20090-2984
Tel: (800) 374-2721; Direct: (202) 336-5510
Fax: (202) 336-5502; TDD/TTY: (202) 336-6123
Online: www.apa.org/pubs/books
E-mail: order@apa.org

In the U.K., Europe, Africa, and the Middle East, copies may be ordered from
American Psychological Association
3 Henrietta Street
Covent Garden, London
WC2E 8LU England

Typeset in Minion and Goudy by Circle Graphics, Inc., Columbia, MD

Printer: Edwards Brothers, Inc., Ann Arbor, MI
Cover Designer: Naylor Design, Washington, DC

The opinions and statements published are the responsibility of the authors, and such opinions and statements do not necessarily represent the policies of the American Psychological Association.

**Library of Congress Cataloging-in-Publication Data**
Silvia, Paul J., 1976-
 Write it up : practical strategies for writing and publishing journal articles /
 Paul Silvia, PhD. — First edition.
   pages cm
 Includes bibliographical references and index.
 ISBN-13: 978-1-4338-1814-1
 ISBN-10: 1-4338-1814-0
1. Authorship. 2. Academic writing. 3. Psychology—Authorship. 4. Social sciences—Authorship. I. Title.
 PN146.S553 2015
 808.02—dc23
                                    2014014381

**British Library Cataloguing-in-Publication Data**
A CIP record is available from the British Library.

*Printed in the United States of America*
*First Edition*
http://dx.doi.org/10.1037/14470-000

# Contents

# Preface

Beginners have a lot of good resources for learning how to write articles: The latest *Publication Manual of the American Psychological Association* (APA, 2010) and related books (e.g., Nicol & Pexman, 2010a, 2010b) are touchstones, and many other books give good advice for people who are getting started (e.g., Sternberg, 2000). These resources are valuable for teaching beginners the basics of what a scientific paper in APA Style should look like, what the different sections are for, and what common flaws should be avoided.

But book smarts only go so far. Street smarts—the knowledge and strategies gained from hard-earned experience—are also needed to navigate the mean streets of academic writing and publishing. How do prolific writers write? How do people who have published dozens upon dozens of articles pick journals, outline Introductions, and decide what to discuss in Discussions? How do they deal with reviewers' comments and craft resubmission letters? How do they decide which projects are worth their time?

*Write It Up* develops a practical approach to writing and publishing journal articles, one rooted in my own experience and the good advice others have shared with me. If you work in an IMRAD field—your papers have an Introduction, Method, Results, and Discussion in APA Style—in the social, behavioral, educational, and health sciences, this book will show you how to plan, write, and submit good manuscripts. Along the way, we'll also consider some issues that rarely come up, such as how to write effectively with coauthors, to cultivate a strong sense of style, and to create a broader program of research. My approach emphasizes writing not for mere publication, but for impact, and for making a difference in the scholarly conversation. Our work will matter more if we are reflective and discerning, if we focus on our stronger ideas and try to communicate them well.

This book is a companion volume to *How to Write a Lot*—an older and hopefully wiser companion, one with more gray in the beard and more tales from the trenches of academic writing. *How to Write a Lot* focused on motivational aspects of academic writing: how to make a writing schedule and stick to it, how to avoid binge writing, and how to write during the workweek instead of on the weekends and holidays. *Write It Up* focuses on the nuts and bolts of writing and publishing empirical articles. I've wanted to write a book about how to write good journal articles for at least a decade, but it took publishing a few dozen articles before I felt that I knew what I was doing and a few dozen more before I thought I could put my tacit ideas into words.

The great team at APA Books, as before, was a pleasure to work with. I want to give particular thanks to Linda Malnasi McCarter, both for her advice and her partnership in culinary crimes; to Susan Herman, for her developmental guidance; and to the reviewers of an earlier draft, for hitting a lot of nails on the head. So many people have given me good advice about writing over the years, more than I can thank, but Janet Boseovski, Nathan DeWall, Mike Kane, Tom Kwapil, Dayna Touron, and Ethan Zell, whether they knew it or not, were particularly helpful while I was writing this book. In hindsight, I can see that I was lucky to get excellent advice and mentoring in writing during graduate school at the University of Kansas—my thanks particularly to Dan Batson, Monica Biernat, Nyla Branscombe, the late Jack Brehm, Chris Crandall, Allen Omoto, the late Rick Snyder, and Larry Wrightsman. I'm still coming to understand much of what I learned there. The graduate students in my academic writing seminar and research group—Roger Beaty, Naomi Chatley, Kirill Fayn, Candice Lassiter, Emily Nusbaum, and Bridget Smeekens—helped to refine the ideas and to mock the many jokes that didn't work. To be sure, I don't imagine that anyone thanked here agrees with all, most, or any of the ideas in this book, for which I alone take the blame.

# Introduction

I had so much more free time in grad school. Of the many quirky hobbies I developed to keep me off the mean streets of Lawrence, Kansas, the oddest was founding Broken Boulder Press, a registered nonprofit that published experimental poetry and fiction. Many people say they like poetry, which usually means they had a Birkenstock-shod friend recite a few lines from Kahlil Gibran at their wedding. But our press published weird and wondrous stuff, from found poetry to algorithmic writing to visual poems. And we always got the same response from our less adventurous friends: Why do people write that stuff? Does anyone read it? Where did you get that awesome saddle stapler?

I closed the press many years ago, but I get the same questions about my scholarly writing from the blunter of my friends: Who reads that stuff? Why do you write for such a small audience? These are questions that all writers have to face, whether they're dabbling in experimental language art or experimental social psychology, so we'll face them in this chapter. Time is short, writing is hard, and papers are long. Why do we do this? What's the purpose behind all this effort? What writing projects are worth our time? What is worth publishing, and what is worth burying?

## WHY WE WRITE

Why do we publish work at all? The answer to that question is easy: The written word will outlast us (Greenblatt, 2011), and our ideas must be fixed and archived for present and future scholars to evaluate them. But why *should* we publish work? What are good and bad reasons for dipping our toes into the fetid waters of peer-reviewed journals? Whenever we consider the panoply of human motives, we feel both ennobled and depressed, and examining motives for publishing papers is no exception. Exhibit 1 lists reasons for publishing that I have heard firsthand over the years. Take a moment to read them, and add some of your own if they aren't there.

All the reasons for writing sort into a few clusters. The first cluster has the noble reasons, the reasons we learn as undergraduates: to share knowledge, to advance our science, to foster positive changes in the world. These are good reasons, and we should resist applying either our aged cynicism or youthful irony to them. Science is indeed a candle in the dark (Sagan, 1995), and sometimes it feels like the sun burned out.

The second cluster has the practical reasons, the honest and pragmatic motives that respond to the realities of scientific institutions: to get a job; to keep a job; to promote your students; and to build your credibility with

EXHIBIT 1. Reasons for Writing, Grand and Scurrilous, That I've Heard Firsthand

- To share knowledge with peers
- To pass the quantity cutoff for promotion and tenure
- To show my colleagues that I'm right about something
- To further our science
- To make myself a cooler person
- To denounce a foolish idea in the literature
- To build credibility when applying for grants
- To get a job
- To help the grad students get jobs
- To get a better annual merit raise, which is pegged to quantity rather than quality
- To advance social justice or influence public policy
- To build a professional relationship with a new colleague
- To avoid looking like a failure
- To show a track record of successful collaboration before applying for a collaborative grant
- To learn a new method or research area
- To outdo the people I went to grad school with, who did better then and got better jobs
- To educate the public at large
- To show I still can do it
- To have fun
- To impress my grad school adviser
- It's an interesting challenge
- No reason—it's just what I do
- It beats working for a living

funding agencies, community groups, and the public at large. Humans respond to incentives in the environment. The environments of most social scientists encourage publishing more and discourage fresh paint and windows.

The third cluster has the intrinsically motivated reasons. Many people find writing articles fun. Most of us will look askance at that one—I usually hear it from people who also say, "All your body really needs is water!" and "Put down that coffee and hop on a bike!" as well as other exclamatory curiosities—but it's a good reason. If not fun, writing articles can be challenging, a kind of mental weightlifting. In this cluster is the writing-to-learn method (Zinsser, 1988)—a favorite of mine—in which people decide to write a book or article as a way of teaching themselves a new area and discovering what they think about it.

The vain and sordid and unseemly reasons, our final cluster, usually lurk in the dark recesses of the scientific mind. Over the years, people have shared with me, in moments of honesty and impaired sobriety, some cringe-worthy reasons. Some people publish papers to compete with their peers; to see if they still have the stuff; to impress their advisers; to prove to themselves that they aren't one-hit wonders; and to feel like a better, cooler person. It sounds sad to publish journal articles to feel validated as a person—some people need a dog or hobby—but it happens. Analyses of the downfall of the notorious Diederik Stapel, who published fraudulent data for decades in social psychology, point to ambition mixed with an unhealthy desire for celebrity and attention (Bhattacharjee, 2013).

## WRITE FOR IMPACT, NOT FOR MERE PUBLICATION

What can we take away from this airing of academic writing's coffee-stained laundry? My opinion is that people may write for whatever reasons they want so long as they recognize that their readers don't care why they wrote something up. Authors are entitled to their reasons, but they aren't entitled to an audience. Readers want something good, something interesting, something worth their time and trouble. Papers written out of vanity or desperation won't win you a reader's respect or repeat business. Think of all the weak papers you've read. Did you ever think, "I'll overlook the rushed writing, tired ideas, and lack of implications for anything. That guy needed a job, so I totally understand about this woeful 'least publishable unit' paper. So, what else of his can I read and cite?"

This takes us to our book's guiding idea: Write for impact, not for mere publication. Early in our careers, when we're twee naïfs trying to find our way in the confusing world of science, most of us just want to get published—publishing anything, anywhere, with anyone would be better than remaining a vita virgin. But once we get a few papers published and the infections from the more sordid journals have cleared up, most of us learn that publishing papers isn't in itself especially satisfying. Some researchers do continue to crank out work simply to carve another notch into their publication bedpost, but as one's career develops, this promiscuous approach seems dissolute and sad, and most people seek something more meaningful.

The notch-carving approach is a poor use of our limited time on the planet. Writing is hard and painful. It can take years to design, execute, and write up a research project, and it is heartbreaking when the article vanishes into a black hole, never to be read or cited. A startling percentage of articles are never cited—up to 90% in some fields (e.g., Hamilton, 1990, 1991; Schwartz, 1997)—a point that should give us pause. If no one reads, thinks about, assigns, or cites your work, was it worth your time and trouble? Would you still develop the project, put in the time, and write it up if you knew that no one would read it? I've had more than a few papers get sucked into science's black hole—some turned the hole a few shades darker—and I cringe when I think about the blood, sweat, and duct tape that went into those studies.

In its darkest, prototypical form, writing for mere publication is asking "Could we get this study published somewhere?" instead of "Is this a good idea?" People who follow this strategy aim for quantity over quality, so the manuscripts they submit look rough in all the usual places: missing and outdated references; a sense of being written for no one in particular rather than a defined audience; being far too long or short; sloppy editing and proofreading; a copy-and-paste approach to writing; and too few elements, like tables and figures, that take time and effort to create. These slapdash drafts get kicked from journal to journal, eventually finding a home in an obscure or permissive outlet. Over the years, people who write for mere publication accumulate a lot of weak papers on disparate, far-flung topics. Many of the papers feel awkwardly motivated—big flaws get a hand-waving dismissal in the Discussion, and the research design and measures don't dovetail with the paper's goals and hypotheses—so readers with expertise in the field suspect that the data come from a half-failed project that the authors nevertheless wanted to get published anyway. Over the years, these researchers pride themselves on a long list of publications, but discerning readers wonder why those researchers crank out so much fluff.

Unlike writing for mere publication, writing for impact seeks to influence peers, to change minds about something that the field cares about. Science is a grand conversation that anyone with a good idea can enter. Whether the conversation group you want to enter looks like a jazz-age cocktail party or a band of rumpled codgers who meet for breakfast to grouse about the dissipated youth, all are welcome to step up and say their piece. Vita virgin or not, if you publish a compelling paper, the major researchers in your field will read it, cite it, argue about it, and have their beleaguered grad students read it. Science has many seats at many tables, and we can earn a chair by publishing work that influences the conversation. But not everyone gets an invitation to sit at science's version of the grown-ups' table, far from the youngsters with their paper plates and plastic sporks.

Writing for impact is trying to change the conversation: pointing out something new and interesting, changing how people think about a familiar problem, refining the field's vocabulary, adding new concepts and tools. The impact of an article is made visible in many ways. People cite your work in their papers; catch you at a conference and mention they read it (i.e., they saw it and intend to read it someday); ask you to peer review manuscripts and grant proposals on the topic, thus proving that no good works go unpunished; invite you to be part of conference sessions and edited books related to your area, thus proving that the rich do get richer; and, at the end of it all, conduct research inspired by yours.

So this is what we want: a chance to change minds and to sit at the grown-ups' table. How do we do this? What do people who write for impact do? This book's goal is to show you how to write a good article. That doesn't mean your paper will tilt the axis of the world of science—unlike pop music, science lacks a formula for cranking out hits, so you will need to come up with ideas that are relevant and compelling yourself. But we'll learn how to get the most out of your ideas. Many nice papers end up underplaced and underappreciated, usually because of common mistakes or a lack of craft.

Our central theme—write for impact—has two hangers-on, two ideas that we'll see throughout this book. The first is to plan and reflect: Writing good papers requires planning, sweating the small stuff, and overthinking everything. Science is exciting, and it's easy for our impulsive side to want to get some data together and get it out there before thinking things through. A little planning prevents a lot of rejections. The second is to be open. In the long run, no one fools anyone in this business. This book appears during a time of unsettling but productive discussions about questionable research practices, replicability, false positives, $p$-hacking, and outright fraud. To have an impact over the long run, the work we publish has to be candid, credible, and open. Some people don't get this. For example, an inane but common hope—and a hallmark of writing for mere publication—is for reviewers who won't notice some flaw that the author tried to mute. Hoping a few people won't see a blemish so that everyone can see it, in immutable black and white, is delusional and self-defeating.

## LOOKING AHEAD

This book develops our guiding goal—to write for impact and thus gain a seat at the table with sharp knives and candles. In Part I, we focus on broader problems to ponder before we start writing. Chapter 1 considers how to pick the right journal for your paper. Many good papers get rejected because they were pointed at the wrong audience. Chapter 2 considers the thorny problem of style. Good writing will make your papers more appealing to your reviewers and readers, so how can we write well? Finally, Chapter 3 delves into collaborative writing. Because most of our work is in teams, we need tools for writing collaborative papers quickly and effectively.

Part II journeys into the heart of IMRAD darkness: the Introduction, Method, Results, and Discussion. Each of these four sections gets a chapter of its own (Chapters 4–7). By stepping back and thinking about each section's rhetorical purpose, we can find some strategies for crafting papers that are interesting, open, and easy to understand. Part II ends with an obsessive treatise on the little things—titles, references, footnotes, and abstracts (Chapter 8). These runty elements don't get the respect they deserve, but impact comes from taking every part of a paper seriously.

In Part III, we look at the aftermath of your paper. Chapter 9 discusses how to deal with journals. Some good papers get rejected because people mishandle the process of submitting, revising, and resubmitting to journals. And in Chapter 10, our final chapter, we step back and consider the bigger picture of impact. Now that your own paper is done, how do you build an influential program of research over the long run?

So let's get to it. In Chapter 1, we'll dig into evaluating and picking journals. But before we do, give me a second to get a clean paper plate and spork.

# I

# PLANNING AND PREPPING

# 1

## How and When to Pick a Journal

The scholarly life is full of vexing choices: Which NPR affiliate should I listen to this morning? Which farmer's market should I buy organic okra from? Which soy-based highlighter should I use to write comments of devastating snark on the wretched pile of papers that need grading? For the scholarly writer, the most vexing choice is where to submit your manuscript, the organic fruit of your fair-trade labor. There are a lot of journals, and more appear every year— one suspects a spooky reproductive process at work, an *eros* of *biblos* in the library stacks after the staff turn off the lights—so it's hard for a researcher to decide which one to try first.

In this chapter, we peer into the world of journals: how to judge them, how to pick a few to be target journals for our papers, and when to pick some. With some forethought, we can boost the likely impact of our papers, reduce the odds of rejection, and spend less time revising and resubmitting.

## Understanding Journal Quality: Great, Good, and Grim

Picking the right journal for your manuscript is like changing diapers—it takes more experience than you would think to do it well. Each field's opinions of its journals are a kind of tacit cultural knowledge. This knowledge gets spread informally: Advisers give the dirt on journals to their students; researchers gossip about their journal trials and triumphs at conferences; and occasionally an aggrieved writer sends an embarrassing but revealing rant about a journal and its cruel, uncaring editor to a Listserv. Being outside the gossip stream, outsiders and newcomers find it hard to know which journals are good and to discern the subtle emphases that distinguish them.

Picking journals is central to our theme of impact. We want our published work to influence the scientific conversation about our problem, not merely to appear in print, and some journals reach wider audiences than others. Even in our database-driven world of downloaded PDF articles, people keep an eye on some journals and ignore others. If anything, the proliferation of journals has made the best ones more prominent—when there's too much information, people will tune much of it out.

So, obviously, we would prefer our work to be in the good journals, not the not-good ones. And different journals attract different audiences, some of which would be more likely to read and cite our article. It thus helps to rank journals, to separate the wheat from the soy, as a first step. One group of ways to rank journals is quantitative. Several scores—impact factors, $H$ indexes, eigenfactors, and article influence scores—are derived from analyses of citation counts. They vary on many dimensions—some exclude self-citations, adjust for citation differences between fields, or account for citation outliers—but they mostly come down to how often people cite a journal's articles in their own articles. Exhibit 1.1 sketches how the most common metrics work. Journals that publish highly cited papers end up with higher scores on all the quantitative citation metrics, so the differences between the metrics is less important than the differences between journals on a particular metric. Impact factors, $H$ indexes, and many other scores are reported in the Web of Science family of databases; eigenfactors and article influence scores are reported at www.eigenfactor.org. If you haven't already, it's worth poking around these databases to see if the numbers mesh with your intuitive rankings of your field's journals.

Ranking journals on the basis of citation metrics sounds superficial, like Andy Warhol's notion that artists should weigh their press reviews instead of reading them, but citations are a reasonable marker of impact. Some journals routinely publish work that gets a lot of attention, and those journals are high on all the quantitative metrics of influence. And some journals routinely pitch articles into a black hole of scholarship, from which no light or knowledge or influence shall

EXHIBIT 1.1. Multifarious Metrics of Impact

- The most widely used metric is the *impact factor*, which is the average number of citations in a year to the articles a journal published in the prior 2 or 5 years. A 2-year impact factor of 1.50 in 2014, for example, means that in 2014 each article published in 2012 and 2013 was cited on average 1.5 times. Two-year impact factors are volatile—a single big hit can cause a spike—so the 5-year impact factors are much better. By aggregating over a longer time window, they are less affected by the occasional superstar article or popular special issue. All impact factors, however, are biased by domain size: Bigger areas (those with many researchers publishing many papers) have more total citations than smaller areas, so the journals in large fields (e.g., neuroscience) tend to have higher impact factors than journals in small fields (e.g., personality psychology). Because the impact factor has dominated citation metrics for so long, it is a big target for editors, publishers, and researchers looking for hacks. For better or worse, a journal's impact factor can be inflated by nudging authors to cite recent articles and by avoiding topics that traditionally get few citations, such as replication studies.
- The *H index* is the value at which the number of papers equals the minimum number of citations to those papers. A journal with an *H* of 205, for example, has published 205 papers with at least 205 citations each. That journal would be seen as much more influential than one with an *H* of 35, which has published only 35 papers with at least 35 citations each. *H* scores are probably more popular for scaling the influence of researchers: Someone with an *H* of 30 has published 30 articles with at least 30 citations each, whereas someone with an *H* of 4 has published four articles with at least four citations. *H* scores have some nice features—publishing a bunch of uncited papers won't increase *H*, nor will having only a couple megahits—but

(continued)

EXHIBIT 1.1. Multifarious Metrics of Impact *(continued)*

they penalize young journals and researchers who have not yet had the time to accumulate papers and citations. The most common $H$ hack is to cite articles at or below an $H$ level—a few judicious citations can usually make $H$ increase (Bartneck & Kokkelmans, 2011).

■ *Eigenfactor scores*, available for free at www.eigenfactor.org, seek to capture the centrality of a journal to the research enterprise. Using network analysis, this method yields scores that conceptually represent the proportion of time someone would spend reading articles from a journal when researching the field. The scores in a field sum to 100, so each score represents how much space a journal occupies in a field. *Psychological Review* has an eigenfactor score of .022, for example, which is at the 92nd percentile for psychology journals. The scores use the past 5 years of citations and adjust for citation levels between fields. Eigenfactor scores have one huge drawback: They are biased by the simple number of articles a journal publishes per year.

■ *Article influence scores*, also available for free from www. eigenfactor.org, reflect how often a journal's articles are cited. Like eigenfactor scores, these scores use 5 years of data and adjust for citation differences between fields. Article influence scores are intuitive: The mean article influence score in a field is 1, so journals with scores higher than 1 are above average in influence within their field. *Psychological Review* has an article influence of 5.95, which is at the 99th percentile for psychology.

ever escape, and the woefulness of those journals is captured in their low citation numbers.

We should be careful not to reify citation metrics. They all have their flaws. Impact factors, for example, don't adjust for the size of an area: A big field, with many people writing and citing many papers, will have journals with higher impact factors than a small field. Because citation metrics are used in high-stakes decisions, such as hiring, annual reviews, and promotion, researchers routinely hack them. Impact factors can be inflated by citing recent papers from journals one publishes in; H indexes can be inflated by citing one's own papers that fall at and just below the H score (Bartneck & Kokkelmans, 2011).

Another way to sort journals is qualitative. The many metrics of journal impact—and their annual swings and swoons—are useful, but they can exaggerate minor differences between journals and cause decision paralysis in new authors. Many journals are too new or too specialized to be indexed by the major citation databases, so they don't have citation scores. The biggest drawback to citation metrics, though, is that they ignore researchers' opinions about the relative merits of their journals. It might seem odd to put opinions over math, but I think that a field's subjective appraisal of its journals is what really counts. Impact comes from people in your scholarly community reading and judging your work—if your peers think the journal is good, then it's good.

My own mental model of journals sorts them into three tiers. The first tier is the smallest: It has journals that everyone in your field sees as among the best. These journals have a history of publishing landmark papers, and the best scholars in the field send their best work there. Grad students who yearn for research careers look at these journals like film ingénues look at casting calls—it takes just one *yes* to get your big break.

The second tier—the biggest of the three—has important journals that contain most of the field's work. The best scholars in a field routinely publish some of their work there, and most of the journals can proudly claim some landmark papers. Your peers have all heard of these journals, and if you browsed through a few issues, you would recognize many or most of the authors and their departments. Some second-tier journals are better than others, in both citation metrics and subjective reputations, and some are more specialized than others, but they all are moving the field forward and will attract positive attention to your work.

The third tier—the seamy underbelly of scholarly publishing—is a spooky place where you should fear to tread. These journals aren't hard to identify. One clue is citations: These journals rarely get cited by papers in first- and second-tier journals. Another is the opinions of your peers. Active researchers have their ear to the ground for gossip about journals, so any journal that most people in a field haven't heard of is sketchy. And finally, these journals usually want money to publish your article.

The explosion of web-based, open-access journals has complicated the issue of author payments. There are many fine first-tier, open-access journals that ask for money from authors: Because they make the work available for free instead of charging libraries, these journals need to get funding from somewhere. The best open-access journals pass all the tests noted earlier: Their papers get cited, they publish important work by leading researchers, and people in the field respect them. But most open-access journals, frankly, are shady, and beginners should avoid all but the best-known ones. A depressing test described in *Science* (Bohannon, 2013) revealed that most open-access journals accept essentially everything and have no real process of peer review. Some third-tier journals defy belief. Jeffrey Beall, a critic of "predatory publishers" (Beall, 2012), runs an interesting blog about open-access shenanigans (http://scholarlyoa.com), such as tales of fake journals that trick authors into submitting by imitating the names of real journals or by hijacking a real journal's webpage.

The three-tier model is an easy way to think about the journals in your field. You want to publish in the top two and never publish in the third. It's better to toss the manuscript into your file cabinet than into the pages of a journal that your colleagues disrespect. A good heuristic for distinguishing the second and third tiers is your inner sense of shame. Would you be embarrassed to have your work appear there? Would you be tempted to omit it from your vita, webpage, job application, or promotion dossier? When your grad school adviser asks why you sent your paper there, would you say, "I was young and needed the money"?

Rejecting the bottom tier leaves us with the other two. You may be thinking, "If the best journals yield the most impact, then why not always start at the top and work your way down?" This is a common strategy, and I know people who use it. They write a manuscript, send it to the best journal, and then march down their mental best-to-worst list until some journal takes it. This strategy has its appeal—by chance alone, a few papers will get into better journals than they deserve— but I can't recommend it. The desire for impact should be balanced against time and reality. Grad students and assistant professors can't afford to waste years in a quixotic sightseeing tour of their field's journals, and we should be discerning about our writing. If you send everything you write to the best journals, you'll seem desperate or unreflective. The editors and reviewers are your colleagues—and sometimes your good friends— and you don't want to appear clueless.

## When to Pick a Journal

When should you choose a journal? This is a question that beginners don't know to ask. The intuitive journal timeline for research is to get an idea, do the research, write the sucker up, and then ponder the options, but this is an inefficient way to write. Each journal is an audience whose attention we want. The pool of reviewers and readers will find some ideas, arguments, supporting literatures, and research approaches compelling. You can't craft a manuscript that influences the field's conversation about the topic unless you know who is doing the talking.

At a minimum, writers should pick a target journal before they begin writing. Defining the journal fixes the audience, so you'll know whom you're talking to. As we'll see in Part II of this book, crafting a compelling manuscript involves many small tricks, some of which involve trying to make your manuscript look like the kind of paper that a journal publishes. You'll also know the nut and bolts of the journal's guidelines, such as requirements for length, references, tables, and figures.

But the best time to pick a journal is before you conduct the research. This might sound odd, but it's a common heuristic among experienced researchers. Research ideas are like Chinese restaurants: They're everywhere, but only a few are any good. It's easy to confuse the appeal of a new idea, shiny and perfect in the way only an untested hypothesis can be, with the value of a good idea. One way to decide whether an idea is worth pursuing is to think about where it would get published. When deciding whether an idea is worth doing, assume that the project works and then predict, with a cold and unnatural realism, which journals would take it or reject it. Would it appear in a top-tier outlet? A solid second-tier outlet? Or would it fall in the large category of "we could publish that somewhere" ideas? If the idea seems to fall in a midpack journal, what might be changed to make the idea more compelling?

Another virtue of choosing a journal before you do the research is that you can craft the project to appeal to the audience that you want to influence. Like fashion and music, research has an aspect of style. Some top-tier journals, for example, want a single tight study, something definitive and fully realized, whereas other top-tier journals want four or five studies, each a small work that builds on the others. Certain audiences want to see a certain style of work—kinds of samples, methods, and measures, the right scope and scale—and it's better to know this before you design the research than after the data are collected.

## PICKING A JOURNAL

Researchers with many years in the trenches usually find it easy to pick a journal—they have the tacit cultural knowledge of their field's journals that newcomers lack. But what are beginners to do?

### Reading Your References

The most common heuristic—but the weakest, in my opinion—is the "read your references" strategy. The idea is straightforward: We can look at our manuscript's references, see how often we cited different journals, and then consider the journals that we cited the most. I think this strategy is overrated because it is biased toward first-tier, aspirational journals. Stronger journals get cited more often than weaker ones in all manuscripts—that's one reason why they're stronger, after all—so this strategy leads people to aim too high. The more serious flaw, however, is that it implies that people should write their paper first and then choose where to send it. As we just discussed, writers should pick a journal as early as possible. Each journal represents an audience, and we can't speak persuasively unless we know whom we're talking to.

## The Word on the Street

If you lack the informal knowledge of your field's journals, then simply ask your advisor, grad student pals, friends, and anyone who seems both informed and relentlessly gossipy. You want the dirt. This is the best way to discern subtle differences in approaches between journals, and you'll get some useful—or at least lurid—information about the peer-review process. Other researchers can tell you how long it took for the journal to get reviews back, whether the reviews were sensible, and whether the editor's rejection letter was accompanied by a baggie of diamond-cut shreddings.

I find myself on both sides of this exchange. I have an unseemly interest in journals, so people often hit me up for dirt and suggestions. And when I'm working in an unfamiliar subfield, nothing helps like asking a friend in that field. Naturally, I'd suggest asking your friends for the dirt in person or via e-mail, not via a social network posting like "Hey, is the *Journal of*

*Funding Agency Keywords* still lame, or did they finally get a new editor?"

## Feature Matching

Another approach is feature matching—does the journal publish work that looks like yours? At the end of it all, empirical social science research has only a few features: methods and measures, constructs, research designs, and samples. These are variables, and journals tend to publish papers with certain values on these variables and reject papers with other values.

Journals don't describe themselves in this idiom, but we can easily classify journals on the basis of constructs, methods, and samples. Many journals are candid about what they are and aren't looking to get. In psychology, for example, the distinguished *Journal of Personality* notes in its author guidelines that it doesn't publish psychometric work (e.g., developing new assessment tools) and that it doesn't particularly want cross-sectional correlational studies using self-reports. Browsing through a few recent issues will show you whether a journal wants only community samples, patient samples, clinically diagnosed samples, samples of children, or nonhuman animals. Concerning methods, some journals primarily publish longitudinal work, research with biological measures, lab-based experiments, qualitative inquiry, or mathematical simulations. What are your variable scores? Once you peg your paper in this abstract way, a few journals will stand out—those might be the ones.

## Imitating Exemplars

Imitation involves identifying a few researchers you admire and then seeing where they are publishing their work. If success in research comes from publishing influential work, then it's instructive to see where influential researchers have published their work. This is a particularly good exercise for beginners, who can get a sense of how to craft an influential program of publications. Imagine, for example, someone who is getting started in psychophysiology, thus fulfilling a lifelong love of electrodes and their many pastes and lubricants. Many distinguished psychophysiologists publish work in two kinds of outlets: domain journals (e.g., journals primarily devoted to emotion, social psychology, child development, and so forth) and psychophysiology journals, such as *Psychophysiology*, *Biological Psychology*, and *International Journal of Psychophysiology*.

Seeing where the top dogs in your field have sent their work may help you become more dog-like yourself. Are the big bow-wows in your field mostly publishing empirical papers, or do they also publish review articles and books? What about book reviews, newsletter entries, and other ephemera? Does their work ever appear in a scary third-tier journal? Combing through their CVs with a grooming brush might not help you identify the one perfect journal for your manuscript, but it will reveal some useful long-term publication ideas.

## Picking Backup Journals

Most papers at most journals get rejected. This is not because most papers are bad or because most editors are broken, thwarted people who take joy in wielding a huge DENIED stamp. The *eros* of *biblos* ensures a steady growth in the journal population, but *eros* of a different nature creates faster growth in the number of earnest grad students and assistant professors who need to publish frenetically. Because it is rational to expect rejection—the odds are always against you—experienced writers plan resubmissions before their submissions.

If picking a journal before you conduct the research strikes you as odd, then the notion of picking backup journals before your paper is rejected will seem like a peculiar delirium. But there are good reasons why experienced writers do this. First, it is in the nature of the professoriate to overthink even trivial things—hence "parking allocation committees." Second, if you pick a backup journal wisely, you'll save yourself the time and pain involved in rewriting and overhauling a manuscript between submissions. It's one of the many obvious tricks that beginners haven't figured out yet.

Journals vary in their length and format requirements. I've seen people write and submit a midlength article (around 8,000 words), strip it down to a short report (around 3,000 words) for a second journal, and scale it up again for a third, as if the manuscript were struggling with yo-yo dieting. Beyond the time wasted in mere adding and trimming, there's time spent in recasting the work for a journal's different emphasis and audience. A bit of planning beforehand, a bit of thought about who is the desired audience and what journals reach it, can avert needless rewriting.

## Wrapping Up

This chapter provided some thoughts on how to pick journals and, in doing so, showed how experienced writers can monstrously overthink even the simplest of writing issues. Choosing a journal isn't rocket science, or even psychological science. Each journal represents an audience. Some want to hear what you have to say; others don't care. By picking a few journals as you plan your research, you can craft your work and your manuscript to appeal to the audience you want to attract.

# 2

## Tone and Style

For someone who teaches in the Information Age, my mental model of learning is quaint: Read some books. When a new hobby catches my eye, I buy some basic books written by experts, practice their advice, reread as needed, and then shift to advanced books as my skills develop. This has worked for baking bread (Hamelman, 2004), repairing mechanical watches (de Carle, 1979), and converting the family lawnmower into a high-horsepower hellion (Dempsey, 2008). I suspect that most academics agree with my intricate and nuanced read-some-books pedagogy, for this is how we learn what we know. Need to learn multilevel models, focus-group methods, or Bayesian statistics? There are books for that—painful books, to be sure, but that's what learning is like sometimes.

And so, too, with writing: I learned nearly everything I know from reading books about writing. I started with the basics, which I still reread, and have ended up reading puzzling books on grammar and linguistics. I don't get a lot out of those books yet, but I'm getting there—a lawnmower isn't rebuilt in a day. But surprisingly few professors and grad students read books about writing (Sword, 2012), and the quality of writing in the journals reflects it. Ignorance never stopped people from having strong opinions, of course, so arbitrary peeves—"Don't use contractions! Don't start a sentence with *But* or *And*! Don't omit the noun after *This* or *That*!"—pass for writing mentorship in most departments.

This chapter wades into the murky waters of style. My goal isn't to teach a chapter-length crash course in style. Head injuries aside, people should motor leisurely when learning to write: It takes years of reading and writing. Instead, we'll discuss a few key topics—the sound of your written voice, some fundamentals of grammar, and a hit-list of arbitrary peeves—that I hope spark some reflection on your own writing and inspire you to read some books.

## HOW DO YOU SOUND?

Hearing a recording of your voice is eerie. Unmuffled by blood and bone and brain, it sounds familiar yet unsettling, as if you were overhearing a grad student doing an uncanny impression of you. Let's take that self-consciousness and apply it to our writing, to the sound of our voice on the page. What do you sound like? A prim Victorian? A perky personal trainer? A wavering and stammering beginner? A congested hippo?

The tone of your writing is like timbre in music, an aspect of personality that readers discern in an instant. Let's get a diagnosis: Grab something that you wrote, read it with an open mind, and then evaluate it on the following dimensions of tone:

- *Personal versus impersonal.* Some writing sounds personal: It sounds like a particular person wrote it, cared about it, and wanted some other person to read it. It has the sound of a human transaction. Be it serious or silly, polemical or peaceful, it conveys the stamp of the author's personality and the sincerity of trying to say something well. Other writing sounds impersonal, the detached feel of writing associated with no human in particular. This is the sound of bureaucratic memos and corporate reports: They feel like disembodied text written by no one for some vague audience that won't enjoy reading it.

- *Informal versus formal.* Some writing shuffles about in beachwear: It feels casual and familiar, genial and earthy. Such writing has the improvisational and vivid feel of spoken English. Other writing slips off the weekend's flip-flops for the workweek's leather shoes: It feels serious and sober.

- *Collaborative versus combative.* Some writing sounds collegial: It feels like the author identifies with the audience, that he or she views the audience as collaborators. This reflects respect for the audience and a desire to reach through the page to the reader.

Other writing feels hostile: The author comes across as haughty or pedantic, as someone who under-estimates or disrespects the reader. A collaborative writer teaches; a combative one wants to set some-one straight.

■ *Confident versus defensive.* Some writing feels confi-dent: The writer comes across as assured and credi-ble. Readers might disagree with the author's claims, but they agree that he or she has a legitimate claim on the material. Other writing feels defensive: The author is uncertain and afraid of being criticized. Such writing often has a strained, trying-too-hard feel or a cautious, hedged feel. Confident writing feels assertive—it seeks to make a point and change minds; defensive writing feels timid—it seeks to stave off criticism and avoid disaster.

So where does your tone fall? My guess is that most academic writers fall on the impersonal and formal ends: The typical journal article, after all, has the dense and crusty sound of a congested hippo. Most writers are in the middle of the collaborative–combative and confident–defensive dimensions, and only a few boor-ish and insufferable writers are both combative and confident.

Your goal is to become versatile, to have control over your tone. A writer who can sound only one way is like a chef with only one good dish. Good writers can shift their tone for different venues and purposes. Because most people sound too stiff, however, becom-ing versatile usually involves learning a personal and informal sound. Even if you rarely write work with a casual sound, learning how to do so will teach you important mechanics and make your formal writing tighter. And once your tone takes off its periwig and slips into sweatpants, it might not want to go back. You'll find that most readers are like you: They would rather read good writing, and they respect people who write well.

These dimensions are continuous, so don't get trapped into false choices like, "If we don't write formally then our articles will sound like middle-school diaries." Imagine each dimension as a scale from +10 to −10, with 0 as the midpoint. As you learn to control your tone, you'll find that you can slide along these scales at command. And you should—your tone should change on the basis of your purpose and your audience. Calibrating your writing, not sticking to an extreme, is the mark of a controlled writer. Here are my opinions about how to navigate these poles:

- Your body of work should span most of the informal (+10) to formal (−10) dimension. Some genres—books like this, blog entries, newsletter essays, and some journal articles—work better when you let your hair down; other genres—grant proposals, progress reports, and some journal articles—demand the austere bun. Most of your work will be in the middle. Even people like me who find it hard to be serious have some stuffy stuff, as Exhibit 2.1 shows.
- For the personal (+10) to impersonal (−10) dimension, you'll rarely want to stray into the impersonal

EXHIBIT 2.1. Within-Person Variation in
Informality–Formality

Writers who can write informally don't always do so. To wit, here's a snapshot of my own variability on the informal (+10) to formal (−10) dimension:

This book is probably around a +8. When planning the book, I thought an informal sound would make writing it more fun for me and more interesting for you. So far, so good, I hope.

My journal articles for journals that are open to informal writing are around +3 (e.g., "In this study, we explored some intriguing implications of our recent studies. We expected that . . . ").

My articles for stodgier journals are around 0 or −1 (e.g., "The present experiments build on our recent experiments and extend them significantly. Specifically . . . ").

My grant proposals are around −3, and my grants' progress reports are around −7—no duct-tape jokes there (e.g., "The experiments completed in the prior project period built on the results obtained in the initial year and extended them in several critical respects").

side of the scale. Even when writing formally, you shouldn't conceal yourself behind your writing. Be they goofy or grim, your writing and ideas are yours. A grant proposal should sound more formal than a blog entry, but it should be just as personal. Impersonal constructions—*One could propose* instead of *We propose*—make a writer sound bored and indifferent. Aim for a range of +7 to +3—make your writing sound like you.

- Abandon hope, all ye who tread into the combative half of the collaborative (+10) to combative (−10) dimension. Your work should be between +10 and 0. Not much of it will be close to +10—writing about mentorship, pedagogy, and professional skills, like this one, will be up there—but none of it should be below 0. We are entitled to our voices but not to our readers: Pretentious, haughty, and patronizing writing is a turn-off.
- Even if you can't yet control where you fall on the confident (+10) to defensive (−10) dimension, you know where you should be. Anxiety makes some people shrink and others puff up, so defensive writers sound either timid or strident. A confident writer, in contrast, comes across as a reasonable person with the credibility that comes from reading widely, thinking logically, and respecting the discipline's norms for scholarship.

## CRAFT

A portfolio of sounds is our goal, but in all cases our writing must exude craft, a sense that there's an expert behind the words with a firm hand on the wheel and a steely gaze on the horizon. Writing informally doesn't mean forsaking grammar; writing formally doesn't mean heaping passive sentences on the page. To gain control over how you sound, you must master some basic mechanics. Most people can write only one way because they are hemmed in by their paltry knowledge of grammar.

**Read Some Books**

The first step in craft, of course, is to read some books. Writing might come more naturally to some people than others, but we all can write well if we spend some quality time with good books. Exhibit 2.2 lists a handful of books to get you started. These are my touchstone books: They are among the few things that the grad students know they shouldn't mock when I'm around. After reading those, buy whatever seems useful and read at least one book a year.

**Snuggle Up to Punctuation**

In most scholarly articles you will find only two punctuation marks: the comma and the period, with the former dwarfing the latter. Ignorance about the lowly facts of punctuation, I'm convinced, underpins most of the ghastly writing we see in journals. Commas and periods afford only a few sentence forms and hinder some elegant forms of subordination and coordination. With only two tools in the box, the writer is limited to building lowly spice racks and trivets.

*Semicolons*

I love semicolons. My love is an intellectual one, unlike Chuck Wendig's (2011), whose essay "I Want to Buy the Semi-Colon a Private Sex Island" says more than women were meant to know about the bond between men and their punctuation marks. One fears to learn what he thinks of the virgule.

EXHIBIT 2.2. A Reading List for Academic Writers

*On Writing Well* by William Zinsser (2006)

    More than any other book, *On Writing Well* will scrape the barnacles from your weathered and crusty style. Zinsser argues for a personal tone, the sound of one person speaking to another. The book is packed with tattoo-worthy quotes, such as, "Few people realize how badly they write" (p. 17). Them's fighting words.

*The Practical Stylist* by Sheridan Baker (1969)

    This book had an incalculable influence on my writing. Baker's thesis is that in style "there are things to do and things not to do, and these can be learned" (p. 2), an appealing idea. I prefer the editions published from the late 1960s to the 1980s, which are pitched at a higher level. Baker's book unleashes some great lines, such as, "All this time you have been writing sentences, as naturally as breathing, and perhaps with as little variation" (p. 27).

*Garner's Modern American Usage* by Bryan Garner (2009)

    Need to know whether it's okay to use *while* for *although* or *since* for *because?* Confused about the difference between *clinch* and *clench?* Unsure if *butt naked* or *buck naked* is proper usage? This spectacular book, an A-to-Z dictionary of usage, has it all. You might expect an A-to-Z dictionary of usage, grammar, and spelling to be boring, but Garner's book sparkles. In reference to hypallage, for example, we learn that "pedants who complain about almost any phrase like the ones listed ('But the marker itself isn't permanent, is it?') are simply parading their own pedantry" (p. 431). Any usage guide with a page-long entry on *duct tape* (vs. *duck tape;* p. 282) demands our respect.

Semicolons have only two common uses and one common misuse. The first use connects two independent clauses. Here the semicolon provides a sense of balancing and pivoting, so it nicely contrasts two ideas:

- A collaborative writer teaches; a combative one wants to set someone straight.
- Writing informally doesn't mean forsaking grammar; writing formally doesn't mean heaping passive sentences on the page.

Semicolons work when both clauses are parallel instead of subordinated. If the second part is subordinate to the first, you probably want a colon or dash. The second use separates elements in a complicated series. If the elements in a series have their own subordination with commas, use a "serial semicolon" instead of a serial comma to segregate them.

The most common misuse of a semicolon is to slap a fragment after one:

- Our experiments used outcomes from both individual and contextual levels of analysis; unlike past research.

When coordinating two clauses, a semicolon is correct only if a period would also be correct. *However* seems to cause the most trouble after semicolons: Stick a comma after it if you mean *but* or *yet* but not if you mean "in whatever amount or manner" (e.g., "However you go, go quickly").

- Study 1 provided initial support for our hypothesis; however, it didn't find the expected mediation.

*Colons*

Most beginners see the colon as a pony with one trick: enumerating a list. You can use the colon for this, of course, but the colon is a trickster. It brings together two elements that are closely related, particularly when the second element elaborates on the first:

- For someone who teaches in the Information Age, my mental model of learning is quaint: Read some books.
- Some writing shuffles about in beachwear: It feels casual and familiar, genial and earthy.

Common elaborations for colons are *general: specific*, *concept: instance*, *action: consequence*, and *claim: evidence*. Enumerating items in a list is merely one kind of elaboration:

- In most scholarly articles you will find only two punctuation marks: the comma and the period, with the former dwarfing the latter.

Colons are hard to replace. A period implies more separation than you want; a semicolon implies parallel coordination rather than elaboration. You can often use commas instead of colons, but the resulting sentences are wordy and stiff:

- Some writing shuffles about in beachwear, **in that** it feels casual and familiar, genial and earthy.

- In most scholarly articles you will find only two punctuation marks, **which are** the comma and the period, with the former dwarfing the latter.

*Dashes*

Dashes—also known as *em dashes* because they are the width of a capital M—are habit forming and probably dangerous to today's sheltered youth. With few constraints on their use, dashes are easily abused. They open up new frontiers in style, so learning the dash is like taking your first trip abroad, albeit with better showers.

The dash has two common uses: inserting and appending. First, using two dashes, you can insert a clause or phrase into a sentence. Dashes licentiously allow nearly anything to slip in, from short phrases to several sentences:

- Dashes—also known as *em dashes* because they are the width of a capital M—are habit forming and probably dangerous to today's sheltered youth.
- Ignorance never stopped people from having strong opinions, of course, so arbitrary peeves—"Don't use contractions! Don't start a sentence with *But* or *And*! Don't omit the noun after *This* or *That*!"—pass for writing mentorship in most departments.

Inserting is hard without dashes. Parentheses work, but they mute rather than emphasize. Commas work in some cases (e.g., inserting a subordinate phrase) but not in others (e.g., inserting a whole sentence).

Second, using one dash, you can append a clause or phrase to a sentence. The appended element can be short or long, a series or a single thing:

- There are books for that—painful books, to be sure, but that's what learning is like sometimes.

Don't combine inserted and appended elements in one sentence—the reader will struggle to identify what is inset and what is appended—like this one—it's too confusing.

You are probably thinking, "Might I perchance combine punctuation marks into flamboyant celebrations of coordination and subordination?" As if you had to ask:

- Some genres—books like this, blog entries, newsletter essays, and some journal articles—work better when you let your hair down; other genres—grant proposals, progress reports, and some journal articles—demand the austere bun.

### Punctuation to Avoid

Exposure to the wide world of punctuation can make beginners giddy and impulsive, but you should exercise some restraint with some of the seedier marks.

- The virgule, usually known as a slash (/), should be reserved for technical purposes, such as marking scientific units (e.g., ohms/sec, miles/hour), pronunciation (e.g., /nt/), and the ends of quoted lines of poetry. Don't write *and/or*, *he/she*, *mood/*

*emotion*, *aggression/violence*, *scamp/scapegrace*, or other hybrids—such hedging betrays your uncertainty about what to say.

- After centuries of obscurity, the ellipsis ( . . . ) came into favor with disaffected teenagers who like the breathy and discursive tone it lends to their inane online ramblings about how misunderstood they are: "No one gets me . . . no one . . . and my parents? . . . whatever. . . ." In their defense, it's hard not to be misunderstood when most of your words are elided. An ellipsis signals that something was omitted from a quoted source. That's it. Don't use it to trail off (e.g., "It's hard to say . . . "), if not for style then for the principle of keeping aposiopesis at home where it belongs.

- The exclamation point is the answer to a rhetorical problem dating to the ancient Greeks: How can you create a sense of elevated emphasis after your long, all-caps rant aimed at strangers on the Internet who dislike cats? I feel bad for the exclamation point, which has been skunked by its association with bad writers who have big emotions but small vocabularies. Avoid it. You will sound shrill and wild-eyed! SERIOUSLY!!!

**Write Shorter Paragraphs**

Some authors can't seem to write a subheading shorter than four lines, let alone a paragraph. They dislike runty paragraphs, confusing length with heft, wordiness with purpose, size with insight. Granted, tiny paragraphs can be unsatisfying, like a teaspoon of ice cream, but that's no excuse for sticking our heads beneath the soft-serve machine.

Sheridan Baker (1969) suggested thinking of paragraphs as "identical rectangular frames to be filled" (p. 17). Our intuition tells us that the natural scope of our ideas determines the length of a paragraph—big ideas need more space—but Baker is right. Writing should impose discipline on our ideas, which are rarely as big as we think. If we aim for four to six sentences for our standard expository paragraphs—the ones in our Introductions and Discussions—the paragraphs will flow nicely. With your regular frames as a backdrop, the occasional huge paragraph or single-sentence paragraph will appear emphatic and intentional, not lazy and accidental.

## Vary Your Sentences

Most academic sentences are ponderous things, clomping along from phrase to clause, from comma to comma to period. Your writing will be more interesting if you vary your sentences. One way is to vary by grammatical type, such as classifying your sentences as *simple*, *complex*, or *compound*. Simple sentences have only one main clause, complex sentences have only one main clause and at least one subordinate clause, and compound sentences have at least two main clauses coordinated in parallel (Quirk, Greenbaum, Leech, & Svartvik, 1985). Most academic sentences are big, complex ones held together with commas and hope.

A more natural way, however, is to vary by intuitive type. Readers think of sentences using tacit concepts like *simple*, *complicated*, *long*, and *spacious*. Exhibit 2.3 gives a handful of intuitive sentence types. Mixing and matching from this descriptive taxonomy of sentences will add variability. A rough but effective test of sentence variability is punctuation variability. If a page of text has dashes, semicolons, colons, and question marks, it usually has good sentence variability. Correlation is causation here: You can force yourself away from a comma-heavy style by using other forms.

Like punctuation, coordination is a neglected tool for varying sentences. Ponder, if you will, how you would coordinate two or more clauses or phrases. The most common form—perhaps the only to come to mind—is *syndeton*. In syndetic coordination, we use a coordinating conjunction, such as *but* or *and*, before the final element. We see syndeton everywhere:

■ This works for baking bread, repairing mechanical watches, **and** converting the family lawnmower into a high-horsepower hellion.

But you have more choices than you think. Another option is to add the coordinating conjunction before each element, a form known as *polysyndeton*. You've seen this without noticing it:

■ Unmuffled by blood **and** bone **and** brain, it sounds familiar yet unsettling, as if you were overhearing a grad student doing an uncanny impression of you.

EXHIBIT 2.3. A Handful of Intuitive Sentence Types

*Short sentences.* Short is relative: For academic writing, a sentence with fewer than nine words is probably short.

*Long sentences.* Long sentences are sleek and vivid when done well—just don't overuse them.

*Complicated sentences.* We've all seen these before. Long, abstract sentences packed with subordination will make your readers suspect that your text has been hastily translated from German. Avoid these unless you're Wilhelm Wundt.

*Sentences with inset clauses and phrases.* These sentences place something within the sentence—either a clause or phrase—using commas, dashes, or parentheses. Dashes emphasize the inset element; parentheses mute it.

*Sentences with appended clauses and phrases.* For an emphatic ending, append a clause or phrase to a sentence. A dash creates the right feeling of delay—try one sometime.

*Compound sentences.* Academic writing often compares and contrasts, pivots and balances. Compound sentences coordinate two main clauses that could stand alone as sentences. They work best when the clauses are tightly parallel in form and structure.

*Enumerated and elaborated clauses.* You can elaborate an assertion using a colon or dash.

*Questions.* Natural hooks, questions work well as the first or last sentence in a paragraph. To hook your hooks, write two or three questions in a row.

*Flamboyant sentences.* If you feel the dark urge to pull off a wicked sentence—one beastly in complexity, monstrous in punctuation, or nefarious in coordination—go ahead. You've earned it.

Omitting the first *and*—unmuffled by blood, bone, and brain—would be syndetic. Polysyndeton reminds me of Steven Pinker, a fine writer who owns polysyndeton like a comfy sweater vest. In only the first few pages of *Words and Rules* (Pinker, 1999), for example, we see several examples:

- "All over the world members of our species fashion their breath into hisses and hums and squeaks and pops and listen to others do the same" (p. 1).
- "Inside everyone's head there must be a code or protocol or set of rules that specifies how words may be arranged into meaningful combinations" (p. 4).

Keen observers of prefixes probably know what's next: *asyndeton*, the omission of coordinating conjunctions.

- Some writers fear runty paragraphs, confusing length with heft, wordiness with purpose, size with insight.
- Writing for impact is trying to change the conversation: pointing out something new and interesting, changing how people think about a familiar problem, refining the field's vocabulary, adding new concepts and tools.

Asyndeton is more common than you might think. For example, coordinating a compound sentence with a semicolon is asyndeton at work. The most common use by far comes from APA Style's rules for citations,

which asyndetically coordinate two or more paren‑
thetical citations via semicolons without conjunctions.

## Be Short and Sleek

We know we shouldn't be wordy. We've been told a
million times, but telling people to avoid wordiness
is like telling them to quit smoking, to exercise more,
and to stop wrapping bacon around their doughnuts.
Wordiness is like secondhand smoke for your readers:
Writers can do what they want in their own homes, but
the rest of us shouldn't have to suffer their bad habits
in public.

Part of wordiness is visual. Visually dense text, like
long paragraphs stuffed with long sentences stuffed
with long words, makes readers reach for the machete,
ready to hack through thorny brambles of *individuals*
and *utilize*. Spacious text has shorter paragraphs, sen‑
tences, and words. The brevity creates more white
space relative to black letters, thus making the page
look less forbidding.

We've already made the case for shorter paragraphs.
Baker's (1969) individual frames of four to six sentences
show a writer in control of the material. Shorter sen‑
tences come from two strategies: stopping and chop‑
ping. Stopping is easy. When tempted to slap another
subordinate clause or phrase onto a sentence, stop, take
a breath, and slap a period there instead. Chopping
takes more practice. Using ellipsis, a method of gram‑
matical reduction (Quirk et al., 1985, chap. 12), you

can chop words and phrases from your sentences. Readers never notice:

- Most psychologists who claim to know a lot about writing don't [know a lot about writing].
- I wear a size medium, if you're making some [T-shirts].
- Even if the viewpoints are the same, only one [of the viewpoints] has a mature foundation.
- Using ellipsis, [which is] a method of grammatical reduction, you can chop words and phrases from your sentences.

Try omitting a lot—see how far you can push ellipsis.

Picking shorter words should be easy, but old habits die hard, with nearly the identically extensive level of difficulty with which elderly habits expire. The prejudice in academic writing is for the long over the short, the oblique over the direct, the abstract over the concrete. Some long words are inescapable in scholarly writing, but most are easily given the slip. Consider choosing *but* over *however*, *people* over *individuals*, *try* over *attempt*, and *use* over *utilize*. I'm not sure why anyone writes *individuals*. Beloved by social scientists, the five-syllable *individuals* is like an invasive species, a hideous snake that gobbles the pretty ground-nesting birds. Seriously, people—or should I say, seriously, individuals—banish it in favor of *person* and *people* and specific classes like *students*, *veterans*, *children*, and *citizens*.

When I read or hear a word that strikes me as interesting or silly, I add it to a document stored on my desktop. Most of them won't find their way into my writing—if you can work both *raconteur* and *cuneiform* into a sentence, send it to me—but some do, and making the list keeps me in touch with English's big menu.

## REFLECTING ON PEEVES

Most researchers who claim to know a lot about writing don't. Instead of hard-earned knowledge of rhetoric and a nuanced sense of why writers make the choices they do, they have a list of arbitrary pet peeves that got flogged into them in grad school: Don't use contractions; don't write *this* or *that* without a following noun; and never, lest centuries of precious science crumble to dust at our feet, write "That book argued . . . " or "This study found . . . " Versatile writers know that these are merely one of several options, so it's fine for writers to forsake contractions or make "No Anaphor is a Zero" T-shirts—I wear a size medium, if you're making some— so long as they know what they're doing. It's the difference between parroting our parents' political beliefs and having our own political beliefs—even if the viewpoints are the same, only one has a mature foundation.

But such choices are rarely informed. Most people who denounce demonstrative pronouns, for example, don't know that there is a name for what they're denouncing. For most, it's just another entry on a musty list of *Shalt Nots* that the elders passed down. Let's apply the cool eye of reason to these peeves and see what we think.

## First-Person Pronouns

As an undergraduate I was repeatedly warned about first-person pronouns, as if they were unseemly characters loitering at the edge of campus. "Your research paper isn't a diary," said one professor—this was the early 1990s, back when people would write their innermost secrets in a small, hidden book instead of posting them to the Internet—"and science isn't about your personal thoughts." The argument against *I* and *we* comes from a model of science that confuses objectivity with validity. By concealing the human influence, such writers hope to make their work appear disinterested, unbiased, and universal.

APA Style later argued for using first-person pronouns, and my sense is that most people are comfortable with them. First-person pronouns make your writing more informal and personal, so they're good tools for controlling your tone. For writing that calls for a collaborative tone, you can use first-person plural pronouns that bind the writer and reader. One form of *we*—the generic, inclusive *we*—refers to the writer and reader as part of a broader class of people, such as academic writers, psychologists, or all of humanity. Another form—the inclusive authorial *we*—refers to the writer and reader as a pair. You'll notice both forms, along with directly addressing the reader as *you*, throughout this book. Many people confuse these *we* forms with the often (and probably justly) mocked royal *we*—when a singular author adopts a plural persona—but don't let that deter you from exploring different ways of relating yourself to your readers.

## Metonymy

You've probably heard someone tell you to avoid describing inanimate objects as agents, particularly *books*, *findings*, and *theories*. This usually takes the form of an exasperated rant: "A *book* can't argue for anything; it's just a book. Did it jump from the shelf and starting chattering away? Only the *author* of a book can argue for something." We're thus told to prefer the wordy "On the basis of our interpretation of the literature, we would suggest" over the sleek "The literature suggests."

What we have before us is *metonymy*. Along with metaphor, its more glamorous twin, metonymy is one of the two higher order classes of figurative thought. As linguists remind us, figurative language isn't an ornamental gilding of literal language: Most speech and thought are figurative (Gibbs, 1994; Lakoff & Johnson, 1980). When beginners want to write clearly, they tend to confuse clarity with literalism. But because the mind thinks figuratively, writing is easier to understand when it appeals to figurative thought. "This theory proposes" isn't literally true, but it has a vivid figurative meaning that is hard to misunderstand.

Metonymy is a figurative device founded on substitution: parts for wholes, features for objects, effects for causes, actions for agents, and places for things found there, to name a handful. Parts for wholes is probably the prototypical metonymy (Peirsman & Geeraerts, 2006): When we compliment friends on their nice wheels, disparage financiers as suits and hippies as long-hairs, or ask someone to get us some numbers, we're using a feature to stand in for the whole.

Metonymy's many forms are everywhere. Consider "I'm picking up some coffee—want some?" This seemingly literal sentence is rich in metonymy: *picking up* substitutes the final act in a long set of behaviors (grasping the cup) for the full set (leaving the office, placing an order, paying money, and so on), and *coffee* substitutes the contained (the liquid in the cup) for a container. Similarly, you probably attend or work at a *four-year college*. The college isn't four years—the undergraduates attend it for four years, allegedly—but the phrase stands in metonymically for a complex set of curricular goals and historical trends. *The book argued* is a classic metonym: Something created (the book) stands in for the creator (the author). (This form is sometimes called *hypallage*, which switches an object for a subject.) Similar examples pervade English, even in our vaunted scholarly journals— Exhibit 2.4 shows some common academic examples.

Metonymy is inevitable—we have minds that structure experience figuratively and a language that's more figurative than literal. But metonymy is also desirable, something to cultivate in our writing. By omitting huge classes of features, it makes writing compact; by high-

EXHIBIT 2.4. Metonymy and You

Metonymy is widespread in academic writing. Like "the book claimed," the following examples have replaced the implied subject (in most cases, *people* or *researchers*) with something else:

> The following examples have replaced . . .
> A glance shows . . .
> A large literature demonstrates . . .
> This theory contends . . .
> Recent research, however, contradicts . . .
> A more nuanced approach reveals . . .
> Our findings indicate . . .
> More attention to assessment will enhance . . .
> The rise of new technology afforded . . .
> A century of thought suggests . . .
> Latent variable models distinguish . . .
> Figure 2 depicts . . .
> The outcome of the statistical test supported . . .
> New metrics of heart rate variability can clarify . . .
> Qualitative methods illuminate . . .
> A moment's reflection, however, casts doubt . . .

lighting concrete features, it makes writing vivid and interesting; and by appealing to our figurative minds, it makes writing easier to understand.

Ease of understanding, this final part, is the crux of it. Most metonymic expressions are so easy to understand that they feel literal. Only the deliberately obtuse will respond to sentences starting with "A quick glance shows," "Qualitative methods reveal," "Empirically supported treatments emphasize," "A feminist analysis sheds light on," or "Multilevel models handle nested scores by" with "What? How can a glance show or a method reveal? What demented glossolalia is this?" Such people should show their readers and the English language more respect. Everyone understands metonymy because our minds think figuratively, so good writers should write metonymically. If your peers and adviser disagree, just say, "But the book *Write It Up* argued for metonymy." If they reply, "No, the *author* of the book argued for it," go ahead and tell them that only my book argues for it—me, I could go either way.

## Split Infinitives

Grammarians from the old-school—the one where students brought their own candles and coal and were threatened with thrashings—had a curious fetish for Latin, believing it to be the root of all modern languages. Split infinitives, such as *to critically examine*, were thus discouraged because Latin's one-word infinitives can't be split. For modern writers, I would strongly discourage you from splitting infinitives when preparing your manuscripts for submission in Latin. The editors and reviewers will mock your twee Latin grammar, and your office mates will snicker at your *vulgare latinum*. But if you plan to submit your manuscript in English, which has two-word infinitives that can be split like bananas with equally tasty results, then feel free to ignore the old-school advice from the 1800s.

## Contractions

The mind recoils at the contempt heaped on contractions. One suspects a Freudian reaction formation, as if contraction deniers type *isn't* and *couldn't* when alone in their darkened offices but then stew in shame and self-loathing. Countless times I've heard colleagues intone, "Contractions aren't acceptable in scientific writing." (They rarely say "are not acceptable.") But why not? Like the belief that kissing gets you pregnant, the belief that contractions are unacceptable for academic purposes is just another folk idea passed down from ignorant elders. Books about nonfiction style and usage encourage contractions, even in contexts many scientists consider formal (e.g., Garner, 2009; Zinsser, 2006).

You should use standard contractions because they let you control your tone. They are pivotal for sliding along the informal–formal dimension, for mimicking the loose feel of personal speech. In spoken English, people avoid using contractions only in highly formal occasions, so text without contractions inherits a somber and liturgical tone. And the mental sound of contractions is milder: They feel less stressed and emphatic. For many common contractions, the contracted form undergoes a phonological reduction—a dropping of sound—that softens it (Quirk et al., 1985, p. 123). The /nt/ sound in *isn't*, for example, usually reduces to /n/ when spoken. Read these and feel how they sound:

- Our central prediction was not supported.
- Our central prediction wasn't supported.

In *was not*, the sharp *t* is preserved and *not* is stressed. In *wasn't*, the final *t* is omitted and the emphatic *not* is avoided.

Controlling tone means understanding the causes and effects lurking in our language. If you want a formal, emphatic sound, don't contract; if you want an informal, softer sound, contract. Always contracting is as feckless as never contracting, but never contracting is the more common foolishness. You're never emphatic if you're always emphatic, so avoiding contractions limits your tonal range.

### Starting With *And, But,* and *Because*

Like most urban legends, the prohibition against starting sentences with *and, but,* and *because* is something people heard from someone who heard it from someone who heard it from a cousin. Strong writers of serious nonfiction start a lot of sentences—around 8% (Garner, 2009, p. 122)—with conjunctions. *But* is a great first word: It starts the sentence with a one-syllable signal that we're changing direction. *And*, too, is a crisp signpost: It quickly signals continuation and elaboration. Because these words mark the direction of an argument, they make excellent beginnings to a paragraph's first sentence.

Writers who believe this urban legend are left with stale and wordy alternatives. Instead of the sleek *but*, they're stuck with the ponderous *however*, a three-syllable word that means "How did my adviser hear about this party? Hide that stuff." And instead of *and*, they're left with paperweights like *in addition, furthermore*, and *moreover*.

Your writing won't sound right unless you start some sentences with *and*, *but*, and *because*. You'll find more use for *but* and *because* than *and*, but all three are essential tools for sleek writing. Aim for starting 5% to 10% of your sentences this way. (I picked that range because people use only 5% to 10% of their brains, according to my cousin.)

## Demonstrative Pronouns

A peculiar peeve forbids writing *this* or *that* without a subject noun. The peeve is communicated via a rant that sounds like: "Don't write 'This indictates.' This what? This theory? This finding? This platypus? It could refer to *anything*. Always be precise." That's how we learn that writing *This suggests* is bad but writing *This finding suggests* is good. The scoundrels in this scenario are the *demonstrative pronouns—this, that, these*, and *those*—single words that can refer to complex antecedents, such as clauses, sentences, and thematic units (Givón, 1983; Quirk et al., 1985). Whereas the twee pronoun *he* can refer only to one guy, the brawny pronoun *that* can encapsulate intricate ideas expressed with large chunks of text.

Could the peevish be right? Demonstrative pronouns would be worth avoiding if they sowed confusion or created needless mental work for the reader. And it's true that demonstrative pronouns appear in challenging texts that require close attention to maintain textual coherence. For example, in Norman Bridwell's (1966) *Clifford Takes a Trip*, a *bildungsroman* of yearning, Clifford the Big Red Dog encounters a barrier to finding his owner, Emily Elizabeth: "And then he came to a toll bridge. Clifford had no money. But **that** didn't stop him." Likewise, in Mercer Mayer's (1983) *I Was so Mad*, an intriguing reflection on anger and authority as refracted through the experience of Little Critter, the protagonist, we see:

> Dad said, "Why don't you play in the sandbox?" I didn't want to do **that**. Mom said, "Why don't you play on the slide?" I didn't want to do **that**, either. I was too mad.

That's like *The Catcher in the Rye* for 3-year-olds.

Don't fear being misunderstood: Give your readers some credit. Linguistics research is on your side. Studies of topic continuity have shown that demonstrative pronouns are easily decoded and understood (e.g., Brown, 1983; Givón, 1983). They appear close to their antecedents, not paragraphs or pages later, so our oft-underestimated readers understand what we mean. If it works for *I Was so Mad*, it will work for the *Journal of Emotional and Behavioral Disorders*.

You should use demonstrative pronouns: They are grammatically correct and stylistically effective. We can understand how they work in two related ways. In the first, situational ellipsis, demonstrative pronouns mark a grammatical reduction, an omission.

We learned earlier that ellipsis makes writing lean and sleek. Demonstrative pronouns can be seen as a situational kind of ellipsis, a form that relies on knowledge that the reader and writer share outside the immediate text.

- Unexpectedly, none of the seven experiments supported our predictions. **This** [apocalyptic, face-scraping failure] suggests that our model should be reconsidered.

In the second, anaphora, demonstrative pronouns mark a grammatical substitution, a replacement of one thing with another. *That* is thus an instance of anaphora:

- Need to learn multilevel models, focus-group methods, or Bayesian statistics? There are books for **that** [learning multilevel models, focus-group methods, or Bayesian statistics].
- A recent meta-analysis, however, found substantial heterogeneity. In light of **that** [finding], we explored several likely moderators.

In some cases, the subject is replaced with nothingness, a form known as zero anaphora:

- Dad said, "Why don't you play in the sandbox?" I didn't want to [play in the sandbox]. Mom said, "Why don't you play on the slide?" I didn't want to [play on the slide], either. I was too mad.

Regardless of how we understand them, demonstrative pronouns make your writing better by improving cohesion. When writers omit a subject noun instead of restating it, they imply that the current statement is closely tied to the prior one. Readers thus bind them more closely (see Oh, 2005, 2006; Quirk et al., 1985). Ironically, people who avoid demonstrative pronouns because they want to be clear are harming comprehension.

Grammar, usage, and style are on your side, so hold your ground the next time your adviser decompensates into "*That? That* what? You could be referring to anything!" You can derail the rant by sniffing and licking Quirk et al.'s (1985) massive book—that will work.

## WRAPPING UP

Like a speaker who tours high schools with slides of sexually transmitted infections, this chapter talked about making good decisions. I'd prefer you make some choices more often—the choice for a more personal and informal sound—but any choice is fine if it comes from an informed understanding of writing. We considered some problems and sketched some guidelines, but this chapter can offer only a nudge. Becoming a good writer requires spending quality time with some writing books, putting the advice into practice, and maintaining high standards. As William Zinsser (2006) reminded us, "You will write only as well as you make yourself write" (p. 302).

# 3

## Writing With Others: Tips for Coauthored Papers

Hell is other people.

—*Jean-Paul Sartre*

No man is an island, but a few might be at-sea land-fills. Professors are rarely driven to rage—ineffectual exasperation is usually as far as it goes—but slow collaborators who have hijacked a manuscript and refuse to respond to e-mailed exhortations to let it out of their brittle, yellowed claws will do it. When I give presentations about writing, I often get the "The killer is calling from inside the house!" question. Usually asked by a young assistant professor—and always asked during a break or after the talk, when the audience is dispersing—the question goes something like: "How do I get a coauthor who just isn't writing his parts to write them? He's had the paper for 8 months, and he won't get back to us, and my third-year review is coming up, and hounding doesn't work, and I don't know how . . . Oh, don't look, don't look, he's walking over here!"

This is what we'll talk about in this chapter: what fails and what works in collaborative writing. How can we goad that guy into finishing the parts he said he'd write? How can we make writing with five people smoother? How can we end a disaster before it drags on further? Oddly, the complement is rarely asked: How can we write well together? What makes a team that works work? How can we set up our collaborative team to be tight and sleek, like a band of caffeine-addicted cheetahs?

## WHY COLLABORATE?

People collaborate for many reasons, and the worst is the unspoken hope that someone else will do the writing. It's easier for most people to come up with ideas and collect data than to write up the ideas and data, so they fantasize about finding their complement: someone who lacks data but can write quickly. This yin-and-yang dream is strictly fantasy: There are people who only collect data and people who only do data analysis, but no one does only writing with no independent research program. But it does highlight the one warning I hope all young writers will store deep in their brains: Weak writers will always want to glom on to good writers, and the most common targets are young researchers who are enthusiastic, team oriented, and too inexperienced to discern valuable collaborations from vampiric ones.

To be sure, there are many good reasons to collaborate. Some projects need a team, like multisite projects, evidence-based outcome trials, and longitudinal studies. Such projects, in fact, wouldn't receive the funding they need unless they had a well-rounded team in place. Another good reason is to pick up skills, ideas, and habits from other researchers. Once you're out of grad school, you don't have the time to take classes and serve as an apprentice. Working with your peers is a kind of continuing education that expands your research worldview and toolbox. But many collaborative projects are things that people could probably do themselves but find more fun when done with their pals. Instead of playing video games and singing duets into hairbrushes, we now design experiments, fret over data, and grouse about bad reviews. The joys of adulthood are many.

## PROFILES OF THE DISCOURAGED: PEOPLE TO AVOID

Who are these wayward coauthors? What are they like? How can they be spotted in the wild?

### The Stretched-Thin Collaborator

Some coauthors foment collaborative disaster because, in their own words, they "are just so busy." Their worlds have two time zones: a crazy time of the semester (i.e., any point during an academic semester, plus or minus a week) and a time to catch up. These coauthors are easy to spot: They delight in telling peers, students, and anonymous passersby how swamped and harried they are, like evangelists for a church people are too busy to attend. Between teaching classes, listening to public radio for appropriate conversation starters, lamenting "kids these days," searching the thesaurus for synonyms for *busy*, and mixing the gas and oil for their old two-stroke Saabs, professors are a busy bunch.

Many professors respond constructively by creating a writing schedule—choosing time to write and then writing during that time—as a humble way of managing their time (Silvia, 2007). But others instead throw themselves at the mercy of a fickle and chaotic universe, which apparently prefers them to complain about being busy instead of to read and edit the manuscript you gave them 2 months ago. It is amazing how long a collaborator can hijack a nearly done manuscript. Waiting 3 or 4 months isn't rare; some people have waited for well over a year for coauthors to get back with mere comments and edits.

I've found that swamped coauthors have good intentions. They would like to be faster writers, and they hope to get to your project quickly. But bad habits, bad time management, and bad writing skills lead to procrastination, which leads to guilt, which leads to avoiding your gentle e-mail reminders, which leads to even more guilt. By the end, such writers avoid the paper because sending it back with only minor comments will affirm what they feared: They're one of those sad souls who needs 4 months to read and edit a manuscript.

## The Enthusiastic Collaborator

Many people have the peculiar ability to inspire others to do work for them. Some are good at coming up with exciting ideas; others have an infectious exuberance and grandiosity. Such people can make disastrous collaborators. Enthusiasm for a research project is a storm cloud on the horizon, an iceberg in the distance, an empty space where the coffeemaker used to be.

Beginning writers might be surprised to hear this. Like all people my age, I attribute their surprise to youth soccer teams that rewarded wanting and trying, not succeeding. Writers should be careful not to confuse the cheer squad with the team on the field. Enthusiasm isn't commitment, and passion isn't dedication. The enthusiastic coauthor's passion is intense when the idea is being developed; strong when the research is being planned; dim when the data must be coded and scored; and snuffed out when there are paragraphs to write, references to find, and figures to make.

I don't want to discourage passion and enthusiasm: A love of ideas underpins what we do in science. But be wary when research passions run high. Enthusiasm is cheap; writing is expensive. Not every sparkly idea is worth doing. No one wants to ask, "So who's going to analyze it and write it up?" when the team is captivated by a delicious new idea. And the exuberant coauthor is secretly hoping no one will ask because the answer, of course, is "you guys."

## The Incompetent Collaborator

If there is a First Rule of successful collaborations, it is probably this: Don't work with anyone who really needs you. A few researchers are weak in most facets of research: identifying good ideas, translating ideas into designs, and executing the design, among many other of science's nuts and bolts. If forced to, they couldn't conduct and write up a project alone, so their only option is to lure competent researchers into their dark and windowless lair. Graduate students and assistant professors are the most common prey.

It might be hard to wrap your head around the notion of incompetent writers with tenure-track jobs and a respectable number of publications, but they are out there. Many of them are alumni of top-notch research labs: They ended up with enough papers as grad students to get tenure-track jobs but not enough training to work independently. Others control access to special facilities, equipment, or participant populations and thus get plugged into projects and tagged onto manuscripts. Such writers often have huge backlogs of data that they hope other people will write up for publication. There is something pitiful about a professor who can't pull off a manuscript hounding his or her graduate students into doing it, but that's what passes for writing mentorship when few departments offer formal training in academic writing.

Of the three types of wayward collaborators, the incompetent ones are the most dangerous. If they can't trick, coerce, or wheedle someone else into doing the writing, they won't get anything published. Desperate people commit desperate deeds, like robbing a bank or hijacking your manuscript, so don't get involved.

## Ways That Work

Circumventing collaborative disaster is not merely a matter of avoiding bad coauthors, although it is satisfying to occasionally shout "Unclean! Unclean! Be gone!" when someone suggests doing a project together. Even good teams of effective and committed researchers can work together poorly. Putting some rules and strategies into place, summarized in Exhibit 3.1, will make coauthored writing work.

EXHIBIT 3.1. Advice for Collaborative Writing

- A collaborative project pools competence, not ignorance. Work with people who have their own lines of research and a record of publishing their own work.
- Ideally, one person writes a full first draft. Two writers is acceptable if the second has a limited role that the first couldn't pull off. The lone writer is usually the first author, but not always.
- If there's debate about the paper's slant or argument, circulate an outline and work it out before writing.
- Circulate only a full first draft of the manuscript. Avoid soliciting feedback on fragments, paragraphs, and sections.
- Avoid passing documents back and forth via e-mail. Use shared network space or file-sharing programs that allow the team to work on the same file.
- Coauthors should comment on the manuscript, but all comments are opt-in, and there's a deadline.

## Centralize Writing

The biggest mistake is to write in parallel. Parallel writing has an intuitive appeal: If each section of a manuscript takes 2 weeks, for example, then having four people each write a section at once is four times as fast, right? It works like this. The team's informal leader says, "Okay, each person has a part: I'll write the Intro, Lars writes the Method, Zoe writes the Results, and the other Lars writes the Discussion. Then we'll compile them and add the references and tables and all that." Everyone nods sagely, and the leader says, "How does 2 weeks from now sound?"

I can respect such optimism and faith in one's fellow humans, but it is more likely to get you a Peace Prize than a publication. Parallel writing has three deep flaws—fissures, really. First, people write at different rates. One person will always end up waiting on the others. Sometimes everyone is waiting on everyone, which sounds more hilarious than it is. All chains have a weak link, and you should find this link before trying to menace the slowest coauthor with the chain. Second, in parallel writing no single person has responsibility for writing, executing, and submitting the paper. Writing is more autocracy than utopia— someone, such as the first author, should be the Chief Writing Officer. And third, a manuscript isn't a pile of standard-sized particleboard slabs to be assembled with a hex wrench. Each part grows organically from another. It's hard to write a Results section without seeing the argument developed in the Introduction; it's hard to write a compelling Discussion without seeing the rest of the paper.

What's a better way? Paradoxically, the best way to cowrite a paper is to shut out the coauthors and have one person do the writing. A paper should have a lead author who develops a first full draft of the paper. It's usually obvious who the lead author should be. Whoever ends up as first author is the natural choice, but sometimes one of the other authors tackles the first draft. There are some exceptions, and minor ones at that. One author might have special knowledge or expertise that the lead writer lacks. It's common, for example, for a different person to write the Results section when it involves fancy statistics that only one member of the team understands. Likewise, for an intricate project, the person who oversaw data collection might write the Method section. In such cases, the lead author writes the entire manuscript and leaves slots for the other person's parts. Ideally, though, one person is writing nearly all of the draft and has responsibility for pulling it off.

**Sparing Sharing**

If you're with me so far, you have a single author who has committed to write the paper and several grateful coauthors who fully endorse the wisdom of having that guy do all the writing. When should the coauthors get involved? Before writing, the group should develop the paper's purpose and scope and consider some target journals for the manuscript (see Chapter 1). If you like, you can circulate an outline for comments, but this usually isn't necessary. The paper's purpose and scope should be worked out beforehand because the coauthors won't see it until the first full draft is done. If there are big decisions to be made, they need to be made before the lead writer gets started.

Don't seek feedback on pieces and crumbs: Wait until the whole draft is done before pestering your coauthors for comments. This might sound obvious, but I know people who pitch half paragraphs and single sentences to the research team for feedback. That's extreme, but the same is true for sections and subsections, like a Results section. Aside from appearing clingy, you're wasting everyone's time and losing the virtues of having a single lead writer.

When the draft is done, the collaborators emerge from their authorial slumber to provide comments, edit the text, and insert their modest writing sections. Don't do this via e-mail. Therein is the path to madness. A lead author who e-mails the manuscript to four coauthors will have five files to integrate and reconcile. It's a waste of time and a recipe for version-control disaster. Instead, use shared network space, cloud-based programs, or file-sharing programs that allow each author to access and modify a single file. This saves you time spent reconciling changes and allows each author to see everyone's comments.

## No Hoarding

The end is in sight: One person wrote the first full draft, the coauthors have been asked to do their worst to it, and one or two took that phrase literally. This is a collaborative pinch point, a window of risk, because one of the authors might hoard the manuscript like a heap of twine and newsprint. Projects often go awry at this point because the sense of urgency is lost—the paper is done, and only easy parts remain. Coauthors thus vow to read it quickly, but the brief-and-easy task gets eclipsed by the workweek's many small emergencies. As a result, the paper dangles in scholarly purgatory, awaiting its final judgment.

To prevent hoarding, use opt-in commenting. Each author is encouraged and expected to comment on the manuscript, for obvious reasons, but with one crucial twist: The comments are opt-in, and there's a deadline. If someone doesn't get comments back in time, the paper moves forward. An e-mail to the team might look like this: "The manuscript is in our shared network folder. The paper will go out to the *Journal of Intractable Problems* in 10 days, so make any changes or comments you might have before then."

It's okay if people don't make comments or changes—you gave them a chance, and one or two people shouldn't be allowed to hold back the research team. (I've done so for projects that came together around the times that my children were born. From what I can piece together of those days' exhausted delirium, I gave a heads-up to the lead writer that I would catch the manuscript during the revise-and-resubmit stage and that they shouldn't wait for me.) Each author made significant contributions to some part of the project's conception, design, and execution, so missing a chance to improperly change your commas to semicolons shouldn't get someone expelled from the team. Nevertheless, coauthors rarely fail to get to the paper within the opt-in comments deadline because the deadline elevates the minor task of comments over the many other tasks competing for time.

## What to Do When Trapped

Prevention is surely the best cure, but what if you're currently infected? If you're stuck in a collaborative quagmire, there are a few ways to extricate yourself. The first step is to pledge to never work with the wayward coauthor again. A collaborative disaster isn't something that can be treated with a quick penicillin shot and a soothing lotion—that burning feeling is a bridge. Your global goal, then, is to resuscitate your manuscript, get it to a journal, and move on with your professional life.

The next step is to identify what the coauthor is failing to do: write text or give comments. If the person is taking too long to write parts of the manuscript, there are a few steps. After giving yourself a mental "I told you so" and promising to have only one writer for your next manuscript, you should engage in the gentle art of ferocious hounding. Many people have successfully used the funnel of hounding: Send an e-mail today, then another in 2 weeks, then another in a week, then another in a few days, and so on, until you're spiraling toward the units of time of interest to cognitive psychologists. These e-mails should be friendly—think poke, not stab.

If hounding fails, and it often does, then the next step is to offer the wayward collaborator an out. He or she is probably swamped, incompetent, or incapacitated by guilt, so it's time to pull the plug. Send a friendly e-mail that gives the person an out—he or she will surely take it. Say that, in the interests of time and momentum, you'll write that person's sections and then send them around for comments and edits.

If you can't write those parts well, perhaps because of specialized statistics or content, you could consider bringing in a pinch hitter. More than a few moribund manuscripts have been revived by adding a coauthor who took over someone else's writing duties. The slow coauthor, in fact, might have a postdoc or grad student who could pinch hit. If a pinch hitter isn't available, then just write a terrible version of the person's sections and circulate it for comments and edits.

But perhaps your situation is an easy one. If you are waiting on only comments and edits, not extensive analyses or text, then set a deadline. Send an e-mail to everyone that says that you're waiting on comments from one last person and that you hope to submit the paper in 10 days. This weak nudge might be enough. If not, then send another e-mail with an opt-in deadline: The paper is going out in a week, rain or shine, hell or high water. And, of course, send it when the time comes.

Chiseling a paper out of a coauthor's claws needn't be ugly. Your wayward coauthor might be upset—such people's poor collaborative styles were tolerated by others, so you're probably the first person to call them out on their weak nonsense—but he or she will probably be relieved or indifferent. Many people have told me that their wayward coauthors were impressed by their speedy, get-it-done approach to writing and became even more interested in future collaborations. It sounds perverse, but weak writers will always want to work with stronger ones, and you showed mettle. But don't stay involved—cut your losses and move on once the paper gets accepted for publication.

## DETERMINING AUTHORSHIP

Who gets their name on the paper, and where? In established teams, this issue rarely comes up. Tight teams have the trust and mutual respect that comes from a history of talking about science while eating bagels, so authorship tends to work itself out. If there's a rare dispute, the paper is just one of many, so it will wash out in the long run. But determining authorship, like most things in life, is mindlessly easy until it isn't—then it becomes a vale of tears and woe and recrimination.

Fights over authorship are another gift that hapless coauthors bring to the team. The same people who take forever to do their writing and to get their comments back are the ones who will jostle and fight over authorship order. People who publish a lot of papers, in contrast, have a more karmic approach: Your reputation comes from a large body of work (see Chapter 10), not whether you were first or second author on any single paper, so the vagaries of authorship are less important. A common path, in fact, is for researchers to serve as first author less often as their reputations develop because they increasingly mentor grad students and junior scholars in the dark arts of science.

There are guidelines for determining authorship, of course, that everyone should read. The *Publication Manual of the American Psychological Association* (APA, 2010, p. 18) states that authors must have made "substantial contributions" to a paper. What are these hefty deeds?

> Authorship encompasses, therefore, not only those who do the actual writing but also those who have made substantial scientific contributions to a study. Substantial professional contributions may include formulating the problem or hypothesis, structuring the experimental design, organizing and conducting the statistical analysis, interpreting the results, or writing a major portion of the paper.

These tasks contrast with "lesser contributions" (p. 18), such as entering data, providing advice about methodological or statistical problems, and aiding in recruitment, although the *Publication Manual* notes that combinations of lesser contributions may rise to the level of authorship. In a valuable elaboration, Fine and Kurdek (1993) explored some authorship issues that arise when faculty collaborate with students. They recommended considering how much students contributed relative to what they could have contributed given their abilities and career stage, a kind of judgment known as *idiothetic* in personality science (Lamiell, 1981, 1987). McCarthy (2012) offered useful advice for authorship specific to research with undergraduate collaborators.

But in my experience, people who cause authorship hullabaloos will make trouble regardless of what the guidelines say. A few people can't envision the bleak, forlorn world in which they aren't first author. A few others, seemingly more reasonable, will sulk and wheedle until they are second or third in a set of seven authors. Such squabblers won't make good long-term collaborators, so try to extricate yourself from the group once the paper is done.

The order of authors is a cultural thing, a matter of social norms. Some fields, like mathematics, usually list the authors alphabetically. Many of the sciences distinguish between the *first author*, the person most responsible for the work, and the *senior author*, listed last, who oversaw the enterprise. Some areas of psychology use this method—the first and last authors made the largest contributions—but most list authors in order of descending contribution. A great option that isn't used enough is to clarify authorship in the Author Note. For example, we can say in the Author Note that authorship was determined alphabetically; that the first two authors contributed equally; that the last four authors contributed equally and are listed alphabetically; or as one paper noted, "Order of authorship was determined by a flip of what William B. Swann, Jr., claimed was a fair coin" (Swann, Hixon, Stein-Seroussi, & Gilbert, 1990, p. 17).

As for the number of authors, that varies even more. On the one hand, we have fields like history and literary studies, in which essentially every book and article has only one author. On the other hand, we have large-scale projects in the physical sciences, in which papers with dozens of authors are common. Within psychology, different areas have different numbers—in part because of the scope of research but also in part because of cultural norms about what constitutes a sufficient contribution.

There's much fretting in some quarters over the rise in the number of authors over the decades. The distant past saw many papers with only one or two authors, often all of them faculty. It's more common now to see large teams that include graduate students—and occasionally undergraduates—as coauthors. One reason for this growth is surely the scope and complexity of modern research. But another reason, I suspect, is that a lot of people didn't get the credit they deserved in the old days. Or perhaps professors back then were simply DIY types who enjoyed making purple ditto copies of questionnaires and prepping the punch cards for the mainframe themselves.

Regardless of why, it is hard for me to agree with having few authors as a value in itself. I know many people who, for seemingly aesthetic reasons, dislike having more than two or three authors on a paper. Such people tend to talk about authorship using metaphors that imply that adding an author diminishes them. If you see authorship as a pie, with a fixed sum of credit, or if you think adding an author dilutes the credit to the others, then you have this tacit model of authorship. This way of thinking about credit is counterproductive. It is better to err on the side of recognizing someone's efforts and contributions—don't hog it. And adding collaborators makes the pie bigger: It expands the range of things the research can do well and increases the potential audience for the work.

## BEING A GOOD COAUTHOR

Our treatise on wayward coauthors might have given you the writing version of medical student syndrome, in which students fear that they have each new disease covered in class. If you worry that you might be a wayward coauthor, that your collaborators mock you for writing as quickly as a two-toed sloth with a three-toed keyboard, you probably shouldn't. But worried or not, everyone should cultivate the ability to collaborate well. Across a career, doing creative work involves attracting mentors, collaborators, and students, so creativity theories point out that the ability to work well with others is a key creative skill (Sawyer, 2011).

As in many other areas of life, the Golden Rule will serve you well. Write with others as you would have them write with you. It boils down to three things. First, do the things you said you'd do quickly and well. Write your parts quickly, get back with comments quickly, curse the bad reviews quickly. Second, cultivate complementary skills that set you apart from any other off-the-boat new PhD: fancy statistics, uncommon research methods, grant expertise, or good grammar. And third, say no when you need to. Good researchers will always respect someone who says, "I'm probably too booked right now, and I don't want to say yes and then hold everyone back." All good writers must learn how to say no to collaborative opportunities: Would-be collaborators will pounce on you like writer's-blocked pumas.

## WRAPPING UP

Hell might be other people, but it should be the people reviewing your paper, not the people helping you write it. This chapter considered some ways to make collaborative projects better. Our discussion of bad people and bad processes highlighted a paradox: Collaborative writing works best when people don't need each other's help and when only one person does the writing. Writing well with others is thus much like writing alone. But if you wrote everything alone, with whom would you argue about contractions and semicolons?

# II

## WRITING THE ARTICLE

# 4

## Writing the Introduction

Just as a journey of a thousand miles begins with a single step, a journey of 6,500 words begins with a single word—a swear word, usually, or a long groan of inconsolable woe reminiscent of whale song. The Introduction is by far the hardest part of the paper to write—at least apatite or orthoclase on the Mohs Hardness Scale, an index of minerals in geology. The Intro poses tough choices. How can we engage with enormous literatures in only a few pages? How do we organize our ideas to make sense and to grab readers? And how can we start it without resorting to a bland first line like "Recent years have seen an increasing interest in . . . "?

In this chapter, we'll learn how to craft a sleek and compelling Introduction. We'll first consider some simple templates, which you'll recognize from articles you've read. Like all good cookie cutters, these templates arrange your doughy raw material into crisp, appealing shapes. We'll then turn to the vexing problem of the Intro's first line, perhaps the toughest line in the paper. We'll learn some good ways to start and some clichés to avoid. The Intro will still be the hardest part to write with these tools in your belt, but at least it will be more calcite than corundum.

## FINDING YOUR PAPER'S PURPOSE: RHETORICAL TEMPLATES

What is your paper about? One hesitates to ask someone what they're writing about these days—you'll always get much more or much less than you expected—but what's your current manuscript about? You should be able to condense the basic message of your paper into a sentence or two, such as: "We're interested in whether personality explains differences in vocational RIASEC interests between falconers and urban foresters" or "Our experiment tested three explanations for the effects of inter-block scrambled and spaced serial item positions on delayed retrieval, thus solving cognitive psychology's last great mystery."

But with that said, what is your paper *really* about? If you viewed your paper more abstractly, stripping out the specific constructs, what kind of argument are you making? What is the rhetorical purpose of your paper? Finding your paper's abstract purpose is much like analyzing literature: When the details are ignored, there's a small set of themes, plots, conflicts, and characters. Tobias (2012) argued that there only 20 core plots in fiction; there probably aren't more than 10 core purposes in research articles.

Here are some common rhetorical purposes. They aren't the only ones you might find, and complex papers might use more than one of them, but these purposes capture most of the research articles in the social sciences. Each purpose corresponds to a template that serves as the conceptual axis of an Introduction. Once you have identified your purpose, your Intro outlines itself according to the template's natural logic.

### "Which One Is Right?"

Your paper's abstract goal might be to pit two things against each other to see which one is right. The first examples to come to mind are epic clashes of theories where only one is left standing, but this is only one instance of the template. You could argue that both theories are right under different circumstances, or even that neither is right and the field should develop better theories. You needn't commit to a victor to use this template. In exploratory research, for example, one theory will probably work better than the other, but you aren't making predictions about which one will win. And this template extends beyond clashes of theories and models. For example, you could argue over which mediator, moderator, mechanism, or interpretation is right—the logic of the argument is the same.

The "which one is right?" template is naturally interesting because of conflict (Berlyne, 1960; Silvia, 2006). This is one of many ways in which science is like reality TV: Even when the game is silly, the audience will crave to know who wins. This template is perhaps the prototypical scientific argument despite being relatively uncommon. Much of our research establishes new effects or extends existing findings instead of pitting ideas against each other. A common flaw, in fact, is for a paper to try to evoke conflict-based interest by setting up a straw man to thrash senseless.

A rhetorical purpose contains a template for your Intro that implies two things: the material you must cover and the order of presentation. These templates thus solve the two biggest complaints about Intros— "I don't know what to cover" and "I don't know how to structure it all." For example, if your paper uses the "which one is right?" template, what material would you need to include? What could you omit? Take a moment—your tacit rhetorical knowledge, honed from years of reading and some painful college classes, is pretty good. You have to cover the articles that first presented the theory and that provide the evidence for its validity. The coverage must be fair-minded and persuasive to your critics: You have to cite and discuss the best evidence available for the theory, not fringe findings from far-flung journals. And the same goes for the other side: You have to cover papers that suggest that it is a persuasive alternative.

For this template, you can usually omit most of what has been published. Because your focus is on the relative validity of two ideas, papers that tweak, extend, apply, or generalize are usually secondary to the point you are trying to make. Some papers make or break a theory;

most simply use it or stretch it, and you can omit most of those. Likewise, weak papers—such as low-quality articles published in odd journals—will not add much credibility to either side of your case and can be omitted.

What about a structure? What's the order implied by this template?

- After a Pre-Intro (see section titled Bookends and Books: A Structural Template), you first describe why smart and reasonable people in your field believe that the first approach is right. Be positive and broad-minded, not irksome and petty.
- If you plan to argue that the first approach is wrong, you next discuss articles, ideas, and arguments that make life hard for the approach.
- You then develop the second position. Using whatever arguments and studies are relevant, make a case for the reasonableness of this position.
- Finally, describe how you will empirically evaluate which one is right.

Here's a variation for cases in which you aren't committed a priori to one of the theories:

- After a Pre-Intro, explain why it is reasonable to expect the first approach to work; then discuss reasons to believe that it might not, if relevant.
- Repeat for the second approach: Make the best "for" case and follow it, if relevant, with the "against" case. Treat each side with the same constructive and positive tone.

- Finally, describe how your research will empirically settle the problem of which one is right.

## "Here's How This Works"

Your paper's abstract goal might be to show how something works. The "here's how this works" purpose seeks to illuminate the inner workings of an established finding. For such papers, there's an effect that most researchers in the field will agree exists: There's evidence for it, and the overall effect probably isn't controversial. But why the effect happens—the mediators, mechanisms, and processes involved—might be controversial or simply unknown. This purpose appears everywhere in psychology. Whenever you read a paper that is evaluating potential mediators or testing mechanisms, you have the "here's how this works" template. This template is naturally interesting because of uncertainty (Berlyne, 1960; Silvia, 2006): We know that something happens, but we don't know why. You harness this uncertainty by presenting and resolving a mystery.

What papers do you need to include for the "here's how this works" template? To be persuasive, your paper must firmly establish that the effect really happens. You thus must cover the foundational studies that first showed the effect and any well-known studies, too. It helps to tacitly remind readers that the field still cares, so you should cite recent and in-press papers when possible. And unlike the prior template, you should try to work in papers that replicated, extended, applied, and generalized the effect—your goal is to show that the effect is real, robust, and relevant. Beyond papers that establish the effect, you would cover papers related to whatever mediators or mechanisms are at stake.

What structure is implied by the "here's how this works" template? Imagine, for example, that you are evaluating three possible mediators for an established effect. An Intro would look like this:

- After a Pre-Intro, your first section reviews evidence that establishes the effect as convincingly as you can. If possible, review evidence that the effect matters, that it affects things your readers care about. To be persuasive, your paper must convince readers that the effect is real and important, so crush this section—own it like something you possess.

- Your second section proposes your potential mediators. Each one gets a brief overview, with an emphasis on why it is (or isn't, on the basis of your argument) a reasonable candidate as a mediator.

- Your final section describes how you will empirically evaluate whether your three mediators explain why your effect happens.

The "here's how this works" template is less combative than the "which one is right" template. It extends what is known and builds on established science. Unlike a "which one is right?" paper, it doesn't usually tear something down or argue for a major reorientation toward a problem.

## "Things That Seem Similar Are Different (or Vice Versa)"

Your paper's abstract goal might be to argue that two concepts or processes that most researchers see as similar have important differences; conversely, your paper might argue that things that most researchers see as different have important similarities. In short, you can integrate or differentiate. This argument is interesting by virtue of conflict and surprise (Berlyne, 1960): An unexpected similarity or difference is revealed, a small spark of intrigue is created, and the reader's sense of the thing changes.

What papers would you discuss? For the most part, you would discuss the classic and contemporary papers that speak to the nature of the constructs at hand. Applications, extensions, and generalizations may be relevant if they illustrate that the field does indeed see these things as similar or different and if they suggest reasons why they might in fact be different or similar.

As with all templates, this template implies a logical order:

- After a Pre-Intro, the first section describes the state of the literature: Give a balanced and constructive discussion of why reasonable scientists believe these concepts are similar or different. The classic papers that first proposed the prevailing view and recent papers that exemplify the contemporary view are essential to discuss.

- The second section describes why you believe they are instead different or similar. This section involves discussing theory and research that implies or demonstrates that you might be on to something.
- The third section describes how you can empirically evaluate your claim: How could someone show that these things are in fact more similar or different than people think?

### "Here's Something New"

Finally, your paper's abstract goal might be to show something new, to demonstrate a novel effect that is interesting, fun, surprising, or useful. Your new effect might have implications for understanding why theories work or which of several might be right, but your goal is primarily to pitch something new that deserves the attention of your fellow researchers.

I think that the "here's something new" goal is the hardest to pull off. The other purposes are inherently interesting: Conflict, competition, surprise, and uncertainty create interest (Silvia, 2006). But interest in this template must come from the substance of the ideas themselves, and many new ideas are boring. If they don't connect to things that people care about, they feel like detached hypotheses floating through the ether, drifting along in a fog of irrelevance. When papers primarily seek to fill a gap, they are often showing something new that doesn't strike people as important. But many of psychology's most influential recent papers use this template. Some new findings are fascinating in their own right or have big implications for theories and practical problems.

This template is the most diffuse of the four: It offers less guidance for content and structure. For content, your goal is to review material that makes your new idea *reasonable* and *relevant*. A reasonable idea seems like it would work. Are there papers from related fields, evidence from applied and policy settings, or observations from daily life that make it reasonable to propose the new thing you're proposing? A relevant idea hooks itself into the theories and themes of a field. Can you show the continuity between your new thing and the field's old concerns? Even though your paper is simply pitching a new effect—a new moderator, phenomenon, or construct—it probably has some implications for the field at large. (If you're stuck, Chapter 7 describes a taxonomy of implications.)

For structure, there's no single format implied by this template—it depends on what you're pitching—but here's a sturdy one that will suit many papers.

- After a Pre-Intro, set the stage for your new idea. What does the field currently know or care about? What would make the new idea useful or interesting? This section forms the backdrop against which your new idea is revealed.
- Next, describe and establish the reasonableness of your idea. What evidence suggests that it is what you think it is? What makes you think it will work?

- Finally, describe how you intend to demonstrate the new thing empirically.

You might have a "meh" attitude toward the "here's something new" template. Certainly, it lacks the spark and sizzle of the others: The content and structure follow less cleanly, and the reader's tacit narrative model is less focused. There's nothing wrong with pitching a new idea or revealing a new effect, but I encourage you to couch your work differently when possible. The other templates more easily evoke your readers' interest and guide their comprehension.

This is another example of why time spent planning research before conducting it pays off in terms of impact. Many low-impact "here's something new" papers feel like the coauthors were tossing ideas around over coffee until someone said, "Hey, we could publish that—let's run it!" If we first think about what we hope to argue and what implications our ideas have for the broader field, we can structure our ideas and design our studies to be sparkly and compelling, not dull and limp. Instead of just showing something new, for example, we could, with some extra thought and reading, illuminate how something works, discriminate between seemingly similar things, or speak to the validity of competing ideas.

## Avoid "Reviewing the Literature"

You can't fake expertise. We need to read everything and know everything, but we shouldn't write about everything we've read or learned. A habit taught in many undergraduate classes is to dutifully and mechanically summarize past studies in the spirit of "reviewing the literature." A common assignment, for example, is to identity a handful of relevant papers and to describe each one in a paragraph, usually in chronological order, before getting to one's own ideas. Such assignments can be useful for training purposes, like psychology's version of rehearsing scales, but we want to avoid this book report mentality in our articles. There are places where exhaustive literature reviews are valuable—review articles, dissertations, book chapters, textbooks, and pedagogical materials—but our goal in an article is to make a point, to locate our ideas within the community of published work, not to summarize what has been done per se.

We don't mean, obviously, that writers should ignore what has been published. To the contrary, our credibility hinges on our ability to use published work, particularly papers that we intend to criticize. In all the templates, the Intros build on other people's papers, but they do so to motivate our ideas, establish our credibility, respect the creativity and priority of past research, provide validity for our claims, and engage fairly with contradicting perspectives.

## BOOKENDS AND BOOKS:
## A STRUCTURAL TEMPLATE

Now that we have your purpose under control—you know what you're really arguing in your paper—how do we put the pieces together? Structural templates provide ways of organizing your ideas. The most common template in strong articles is what I call *bookends-and-books*. This template has two small sections—one at the start, one at the end—that bookend the Introduction's main material. And the main material is split into two to five major headings, the books. Here's how this works.

## The Pre-Intro Bookend

Don't jump right into your material—step back and place your research in context. Your Introduction should have its own Intro, something I call a Pre-Intro or an Intro-to-the-Intro. This brief section—usually one or two paragraphs, rarely more than three—foreshadows your paper's main purpose. When you prefigure your arguments, your readers will know what you plan to say. And as the saying goes, it's easier to learn something when you already know it.

To see the value of a Pre-Intro, think back to the last so-so article you read. A typical weak article might begin by reviewing a theory and some studies related to it. After a couple pages, you start to wonder where the paper is going and why the authors are discussing this theory. Are they going to criticize it, defend it, extend it, or apply it? The paper feels mushy and pointless until you eventually learn that the authors are criticizing some aspect of the theory and hope to improve on it; you then need to reread the preceding material because you didn't read it with a "there's something wrong with this theory" lens. Without an early framework, you lack the mind-set needed to understand the work.

A good Pre-Intro starts globally and funnels into a specific statement about the research. The Pre-Intro should start generally, pointing to a problem, controversy, or idea that motivates the research. After briefly describing the paper's main ideas, it ends with a description of what the present work does and how it contributes. Ending with a statement about the research—a specific hypothesis, finding, or goal—tells the reader what to expect and sets the stage for the Intro.

## The Books

After the Pre-Intro, you have the heart of the Intro—two to five major sections that lay out your argument and discuss past research that is relevant to it. You should identify these sections with headings, particularly a heading after the Pre-Intro. Headings mark major shifts in direction, so they mark the road you want the reader to follow.

Your major sections, your two to five books, will follow from your rhetorical template. None of the sections will be a "literature review" per se, but all the sections will engage with past research. Earlier, we saw how each template implies a series of things to talk about. The "which one is right?" template, for example, implies discussing the first camp and its evidence, the second camp and its evidence, and your new arguments. Each of these is a book, a heading. Simply follow the topics implied by your rhetorical template, giving each a heading, and your Intro will outline itself.

## The Present-Research Bookend

After your books comes the final bookend, usually labeled with a heading such as "The Present Research" or "The Present Experiments." This section—usually one to four paragraphs—brings it all back home. Your Pre-Intro set the stage for your work with a snapshot of your problem; your books described the theories and research needed to justify and motivate your research. Now you need to describe how your research accomplishes its purpose: how it shows which one is right, how something works, whether things are similar or different, or if something new truly happens. Your concluding section looks ahead to your research: It foreshadows your study and explains how it can address your major question. In the spirit of all endings being beginnings, your Present Research section both resolves your Intro and prefigures your Method.

The most common flaw of a Present Research section is being too long. Unless you have a freakishly large number of experiments, this section should be crisp, like the coda to a song or the dénouement to a dramatic arc. Writers often try to stuff in material that belongs among the books, like lengthy justifications for using a method or past research relevant to a theoretical conflict. If you find this section growing beyond four paragraphs, you might be trafficking in ideas best presented as a book in the main Intro.

## Why This Structural Template Works

The structural template we have described follows an ancient arc, one found in storytelling, music, and literature since humans started caring if their audience paid attention. Nothing is more atavistic in storytelling than *beginning*, *middle*, and *end*: readers, editors, and reviewers innately get this. Hooking your ideas into this structure makes your complicated ideas easier to understand. You start with a beginning—your Pre-Intro—that situates the work. Your Pre-Intro is like the classical Greek prologue, which told the audience the history, mythology, and plot details that allowed them to understand the play that followed. After a middle that develops an idea over time, there's an ending—your Present Research section—that concludes the major themes, like a musical coda that both recaps and resolves the preceding ideas. Don't fight tacit narrative models that have worked since the dawn of humanity—give your Intro a beginning, middle, and end.[1]

---

[1] If you will pardon a self-conscious intrusion, you can flip through this book and see that it follows a bookends-and-books structure. Within each chapter, there are two bookends—an introductory section (1–3 paragraphs) and a wrapping-up section (1 paragraph)—and three to five major headings, the books. You probably didn't consciously notice the structural parallelism across the chapters, but it nevertheless makes the book easier to read.

# START STRONG

Starting a paper is hard. Feeling uncertain and awkward, writers step into their Intro like a landlubber steps into a boat. Most Intros thus start with a hesitant first sentence, a placeholder for a better sentence that never gets written. I'll call out three flat lead-ins here, but don't feel bad if you have used them. I have in my earlier papers, and we can charitably view this as one of our many youthful indiscretions best not shared with the grad students.

## Weak Openers

The most listless start is the *There is an increasing interest in . . .* opener. This line has some variations—"The literature on [whatever] has shown a renewed focus on . . . " or "In recent years, psychologists have focused their efforts on [something] . . . "—and it is usually followed by a dense thicket of citations that ostensibly prove that, yes, there is an increasing interest in the topic. Don't do it. Saying that people are interested in something never made a reader interested in it.

The second limp opener is the *unfilled-gap* sentence. The opposite of the increasing-interest lead, this first line begins a paper by pointing out that nothing is known about the topic. It often sounds like: "To date, little attention has been paid to the issue of [something people do]" or "A review of the extant literature on [your topic] reveals a dearth of knowledge about [something dearthy]." Authors sometimes use this line by contrast: "Although [important topic] has been extensively studied, little is known about [obscure thing I'm studying]." This opener invites reflexive mockery—people usually reply with a snarky "Maybe there's a reason why no one is studying it." Spark plugs, fossil records, and front teeth can have important gaps; your first sentence shouldn't.

Our third and final opener—and the most insidious—is the *dictionary* opener, in which the first line provides a banal definition from a reference book. You might scoff, thinking that this lead is the province of undergrad class papers. Articles rarely start with a quote from Webster's dictionary, but thousands have started with definitions from the *DSM* (*Diagnostic and Statistical Manual of Mental Disorders*, published by the American Psychiatric Association), ICD (International Classification of Diseases), CDC (Centers for Disease Control and Prevention), or other three-letter words. Clinical psychology journals are particularly susceptible to the definition pox: The typical articles start with "According to the *DSM* . . . " or with a rote recital of a disorder's prevalence rates and key symptoms. The dictionary start is overdone and tacky, the social science version of starting an essay with "If an anthropologist from Mars visited the American Psychological Association convention, what would they think?" And your paper probably isn't about the definition of something or the prevalence of something. You might need to define something somewhere in your paper, but the first line of the Pre-Intro is a poor place to do it. Consider defining it in the first paragraph of the Intro's first book instead.

## Strong Openers

So how should you start? You have three choices; Exhibit 4.1 gives examples of all three in action. One

---

EXHIBIT 4.1. And So It Began: Examples of First Lines From Published Articles

**Questions**
"What should you do when intuition tells you one thing and rational analysis another? How should you choose, in other words, when there is a conflict between your head and your gut?" (Inbar, Cone, & Gilovich, 2010, p. 232)

"When we are intentionally trying to learn new materials, how do we decide which materials to study first? And do we make decisions that are relatively optimal, or do we tend to regulate study inefficiently?" (Dunlosky & Ariel, 2011, p. 899)

**Global Assertions**
"We live in a world where almost all movies are produced in full color." (Chen, Wu, & Lin, 2012, p. 40)

"The ability to automatically and implicitly detect complex and noisy regularities in our environment is a fundamental aspect of human cognition." (Kaufman et al., 2010, p. 321)

"Developmental researchers assess what infants know on the basis of measures of what infants do." (Franchak & Adolph, 2012, p. 1254)

---

*(continued)*

EXHIBIT 4.1.  And So It Began: Examples of First Lines
From Published Articles (*continued*)

"People are most creative when they are intrinsically motivated, valuing creativity for its own sake." (Zabelina, Felps, & Blanton, 2013, p. 112)

**Intriguing Revelations**
"Imagine a wine glass. Is it tall or short? Wide or narrow? Do you imagine it from the side, from above, or is it just there?" (Glazek, 2012, p. 155)

"In 2009, Bernie Madoff pleaded guilty to bilking investors out of an unprecedented US$65 billion in a massive Ponzi scheme." (Rotella, Richeson, Chiao, & Bean, 2013, p. 115)

"If empirical research is to be trusted, you almost certainly have listened to music today and are probably listening to music right now." (Silvia & Nusbaum, 2011, p. 208)

option is to start with a question. Many writers are reluctant to do this, I have found—it strikes them as obvious and pedantic. But starting with a question is an easy and intuitive way to glide into an Intro. From the outset, the reader learns the problem that animates your work, and it is hard to avoid reading the sentence that follows. If you're feeling brash, use two or three questions in a row—you can pull it off. To encourage you to stretch, both examples in Exhibit 4.1 start with two linked questions. Dunlosky and Ariel (2011), revealing a refined sense of style, kick it up a notch by starting their second sentence with *and* (see Chapter 2).

Your second option is to start with a general assertion. This provides a global background for your Pre-Intro, which can then funnel naturally toward a concrete description of your research. They could be funny, snarky, and sly, but these openers are usually straight. Exhibit 4.1 lists several examples. Notice that these aren't glamorous, but they are interesting and much better than an unfilled-gap or dictionary-definition opener.

A third option—perhaps the hardest to pull off—is to intrigue the reader by slowly revealing your purpose. This kind of lead is sometimes called an *oblique start* (you begin with seemingly tangential information) or a *sidestep start* (you start a few steps away from your main point and then move toward it). This approach affords the most creativity and interest, and it's the hardest to pull off. Exhibit 4.1 shows that there are a few flavors to this start. One flavor uses a concrete example, either real or hypothetical, and then connects it to the abstract concepts being studied. Another flavor starts with a seemingly unrelated idea and then reveals how it is connected after all. This lead intrigues readers— "Where are they going with this?"—and creates a satisfying mental click when the connections appear.

## WRITING SHORT-REPORT INTRODUCTIONS

What about short papers? So far we've considered how to write the standard Introduction: a substantial section, perhaps six or more manuscript pages, with headings and subheadings. If you are writing a short report or work in a field that prides itself on getting to the point, you can use the same templates and tricks—with a few modifications. The rhetorical templates are the same—you are making the same abstract point, just in a shorter format—but your structural template will vary. If your Intro is under four manuscript pages, you rarely need headings and subheadings. Instead of writing a Pre-Intro section, you can start the Intro globally and get quickly into the body of the text. In lieu of a "The Present Research" heading, start the last paragraph before the Method with something like "In the present research . . . " and present your material there.

## WRAPPING UP

Many people have told me of the horrible sinking feeling they get when they face the Intro. With a good Method and Results in the can, they reluctantly turn to face the Intro's gaping void, feeling that "sick sense of failure" that John Steinbeck said he got when he started a new novel (Steinbeck, 1962, p. 23). But an Intro is much easier when you reject the chaos of winging it in favor of the structure of templates. If you can identify your abstract point, you can harness the nefarious force of rhetorical and structural templates. These templates streamline your Intro, sharpen its persuasive force, and present material in the form that readers expect.

# 5

## Writing the Method

Most things in life are harder than they look, but some are easier. Making bread, for example, is pretty easy. Mix the ingredients together, knead everything until it looks like dough (and you look like a yeasty Sasquatch), let it sit, shape it, and bake it. That will get you bread that will impress your friends and neighbors, none of whom has considered that ancient peoples made bread with nothing but rocks, twigs, and fire, so we can surely make better bread—especially if we buy an "Artisan Rocks and Twigs" set off the Internet.

The Method section is easier than it looks. It's the only part of a manuscript, I think, that is objectively easy. It's hard to mess up, just as homemade bread and spaghetti are hard to mess up. But all humble things can be elevated to the level of art with a few extra steps, a pinch of obsessiveness, and a heaping dose of overthinking the arcana and minutiae (e.g., Hamelman, 2004). This chapter will help you obsess and overthink your way to a Method section with a crispy crust and spongy crumb.

# A COMPELLING METHOD

What makes a Method section good? What elevates it from home spaghetti to restaurant spaghetti? We don't want a merely descriptive Method section, one that spreads the bland facts on a blanket and hopes that passersby stop. We want a compelling Method, one that convinces the reader of something. Good writing won't compensate for poor science, of course—as we argued earlier, no one will fool anyone. To convince our sophisticated readers, many of whom are world-class methodologists and most of whom know more than we do about our field, we must execute the study well and write it up well.

In the most global sense, we hope to convey that what we did was apt and effective: The sample, design, procedures, and measures collectively afford a test of the ideas developed in the Introduction. To do this, a Method should convey one of two things: The research was methodologically traditional or methodologically innovative. The tradition-versus-innovation axis is a basic dimension of a Method section. Most projects use traditional methods: They are tried-and-true, old-school, and off-the-shelf. But some projects mint new measures and develop new procedures: They are clever, offbeat, and creative.

It doesn't matter if your work is traditional or innovative so long as the Method conveys that it is one or the other. For a traditional method, the goal is to get across that "the methods we used are basically what everyone uses." For an innovative method, the goal is to get across that "the methods we used are new and clever—they do something that past methods don't." In short, the nuts and bolts of your research should strike the reader as staid and inoffensive, clever and appealing, or both.

Pitching your Method is easy to do. For traditional methods, anchor what you did in past published work. First, cite and briefly discuss evidence for the validity of your approach. Most procedures, tasks, and outcomes have a methodological literature that can be mined. You probably already know it well because there must have been some reason why you did what you did. Second, point out that other people did what you did. Other scientists have used your tasks, instructions, sampling approach, and outcome measures, so point that out to reviewers who are not as thoroughly steeped or stewed in the literature. Ideally, cite examples from prominent researchers who published work with those methods in your target journal.

It seems superficial to point out that you're just going along with the crowd. Popularity, after all, isn't an argument for the validity of your work or a good reason for doing something. You can almost hear your mom chiding you, "Oh, so if everyone else measured behavioral tendencies toward bridge-jumping using an ad hoc self-report short form, would you?" But scientists run in packs—which are like herds and flocks, only cooler sounding.

For innovative methods, you'll need to be more detailed. Traditional methods can often be justified with a few apt citations to past work. Innovative methods, however, need a candid discussion of how they were developed and why they are worth using. This shouldn't be hard. Just explain why something new is needed. What does the new thing do that the old thing doesn't? Is it more efficient (in time, personnel, or cost) or more effective (in reliability and validity), or does it do something qualitatively different from the old ways? If possible, anchor your new methods in similar past work. There might be something analogous—perhaps whatever inspired your new methods—that you can point to as your new baby's commonplace cousin. However you describe your innovative method, don't be bashful: Sell that thing.

## HOW MUCH DETAIL?

How much detail should your Method have? One school of thought is that your Method should be detailed enough that other people can replicate your work. Unless you make scale models of lost civilizations in your attic, few humans can generate or tolerate such an excruciating amount of detail. Anyone who has executed a research project knows that too much happened to convey. Exhibit 5.1, for example, lists some true tales—most from my work, a few from friends—that never made it into a Method section. What the experimenters wore, the Rorschach stains on the lab carpet, the amount of grime on the keyboards: Such facts fade into history.

EXHIBIT 5.1. Sentences From the Cutting Floor

- The first 16 cases were excluded because the experimenter, a young female, wore a tight midriff shirt that said "Porn Star" while running subjects. Because the research concerned the role of religious fundamentalism in prejudice against marginalized groups, we thought it best to omit these cases.

- The loud thumping noise heard on many of the audiotapes turned out to be the experimenter listlessly tossing a ball against the participant's wall.

- One child was excluded from analysis because the undergraduate research assistant running the session used profanity several times. In her defense, she seemed inebriated—the research assistant, not the child.

- An unusually large proportion of participants were female, even by the standards of research conducted with undergraduate participant pools, and the proportion increased across the semester, which ran counter to the usual trend. We asked the experimenter—an Australian underwear model on a study abroad—for insight into this, but he had no suggestions.

- Participants completed the questionnaires using MediaLab survey software run on old computers scavenged from the bowels of the university's surplus warehouse. Approximately 38% of the participants were younger than the computers.

- One participant was unable to participate in the masked visual priming part of the experiment because of congenital blindness.

- Most participants were run in the same room, but eight were run in a different room after a participant with stinky feet rendered the main room uninhabitable.

The stronger approach is to provide the information needed for sophisticated readers to evaluate your work. This is the position of the *Publication Manual of the American Psychological Association* (APA, 2010): "A complete description of the methods used enables the reader to evaluate the appropriateness of your methods and the reliability and validity of your results" (p. 29). The goal, then, is to expose the nuts and bolts of your study so that readers can decide if your approach was sensible in light of your aims. It helps to recall our "you can't fool anyone theme." If there's some aspect of your methods that makes you wince, the reviewers will spot it and wince, too. Be open about what you did and make the best case you can for why your methods mesh with your aims.

Nevertheless, it's hard sometimes to know what your readers want to know. Details that are crucial to one field are immaterial to others. In psychology articles, for example, researchers rarely report the dates when the data were collected. (One suspects that some researchers omit this because they fear revealing that they first analyzed the data using SPSS/PC+ while listening to their *Purple Rain* LP.) It's a shame, perhaps, because all users of undergraduate research pools know that the pool varies across the semester: The conscientious people show up in the early weeks, and the impulsive people wait until the end (Stevens & Ash, 2001; Witt, Donnellan, & Orlando, 2011). Other fields, however, require researchers to specify when and where the research took place (e.g., fields that use the

CONSORT guidelines; Schulz, Altman, Moher, & the CONSORT Group, 2010). As another example, it's rare to see aspects of the data collection environment described, such as lighting, furnishings, and temperature. In research on how drinking water improves mental performance—the coffee-hating water types appear to be on to something—it's common to see the ambient temperature reported (e.g., Benton & Burgess, 2009). But you never see the room's temperature reported in most lab studies, probably because the temperatures in most college buildings swing as wildly as preschoolers on a playground.

As with most vexing decisions, choices about Method details can be made by consulting published articles in your target journal. The journal's editors hounded those authors to add, expand, and delete, so published papers capture the details that the editors wanted to see to evaluate the research. When in doubt, you should err on the side of more detail. Ideally, you could post the study's materials in an online archive, an option we discuss later. Reviewers and readers interested the project's arcana could consult the online files, and the rest would get the concise printed version.

## THE METHOD SUBSECTIONS

A Method section is always split into subsections with subheadings. A few subheadings appear in all papers, but some are unique to a research field. Follow local norms: Use papers from your target journals as models.

### Participants (and Design)

The first subheading is *Participants* or *Participants and Design*. The section starts with a description of the sample. Who took part? How many people dropped out? How many people were excluded from analysis, and for what reasons? From where were they recruited? If you have an experimental design—a classic $2 \times 2$ lab experiment or an intervention trial, for example—you would describe the design and the nature of assignment to condition at the end of this section.

There's monstrous variability in how different fields of research describe their participants. One the one end, some fields mention only the total number of people and the number of men and women. This is typically found in social psychology and cognitive psychology, which often recruit undergraduate students to take part in their research. On the other end, some fields provide extensive demographic information about people who were contacted but declined to participate, people who initiated participation but dropped out, and people who completed the study. This information usually appears presented in a table packed with demographic information or a recruitment chart. Describing your sample is a touchier issue than it might sound, so browse a few issues of your target journal and see how published papers did it. If in doubt, err on the side of detail.

## Procedure

All manuscripts will have a *Procedure* subheading, for the subsection that describes what happened. For some studies, the Procedure has only a few sentences that point out that people showed up, gave informed consent, and filled out a bunch of questionnaires. For other studies, the section reads like a script for nerdy dinner theater, with deception, cover stories, and confederates. In all cases, simply describe what happened. Most of your readers are sophisticated researchers who do similar research, so you needn't belabor the details. If you have a lengthy procedure, consider subheadings for describing independent variables, waves or time points, recruiting and sampling procedures, or anything else complex enough to deserve its own piece of the procedure.

A compelling description of your procedures involves two things: reasons and citations. Weaker procedures sections are descriptive: They list what the researchers did but fail to explain why they did it. When possible, briefly explain why you used a task, paradigm, or process. This can be as simple as noting that the paradigm is the most widely used, that recent work provides strong evidence for its validity, or that it is the most efficient. Whatever your reasons, note them and back them up with citations to good papers, ideally ones published in your target journal.

## Apparatus

An Apparatus subsection describes any equipment or software that would be unfamiliar to the paper's sophisticated readers. Few papers need one: Most research paraphernalia is mundane, at least to fellow researchers. You probably needn't write, "People completed the questionnaires using eraser-tipped pencils (Ticonderoga, #2 Medium Soft Lead), which had been prepared by the experimenter using X-Acto 1800 Series electric sharpeners." But if equipment is central to your work, or if you used something unusual for your field—perhaps a shock machine built in your basement out of duct tape, hair spray, and stolen copper gutters—describe it in detail and cite its source.

**Measures and Outcomes**

If you did research, you probably measured something. Describing your measures and outcomes is easy to do well, which is good, because poor descriptions raise the ire of reviewers far out of proportion to the nature of the crime. One suspects that some people lack meaningful goals in their lives if they are moved to fury by your failure to mention scale anchors for a self-report scale, but such is scholarly publishing.

Your measures and outcomes could be anything: observational data, eye tracking, biological samples, clinical interviews, physiological measures, response times and error rates, open-ended speech and text, and self-report scales, to name a handful. In all cases, you need to describe how you measured what you measured and make a case for it by citing evidence for reliability and validity. It doesn't take much space—a few good citations usually suffice. For innovative measures, much more must be said; for common measures, a brief description and a couple citations will do the trick. If your outcome is uncommon in your target journal, you should spend more time describing the nuts and bolts of the assessment.

Self-report scales might be the most common measures, and they are easy to describe persuasively. First, describe and cite the scale. What does it ostensibly measure? How many items does it have? What is the response scale (e.g., 0 to 5, 1 to 7, −3 to 3)? What are the response labels or anchors, if any? Second, briefly describe and cite evidence for validity and reliability. Finally, cite recent uses of the scale in good journals to establish that your work is part of the herd, which is also known as "consistent with best practices." (As an aside, reviewers who are sophisticated in measurement know that a scale per se isn't reliable or valid, but research can provide evidence for the reliability and validity of its scores. You risk their considerable wrath by saying a "scale has been validated.")

## OPENNESS, SHARING, AND ARCHIVING

Psychology is currently in a period of soul searching about how it describes what it does. The introspection comes from many sources. The APA's promotion of reporting standards, described in the Sixth Edition of the *Publication Manual of the American Psychological Association* (APA, 2010) and in a fine book by Harris Cooper (2010), is the most positive source. The aim of this effort is to make research more cumulative, open, and reader-friendly, all good goals. A grimmer source is psychology's renewed concern about false positives plaguing our journals (Simmons, Nelson, & Simonsohn, 2011; Murayama, Pekrun, & Fiedler, 2014). More findings than we thought—particularly short papers that report a single flashy effect (Ledgerwood & Sherman, 2012)—simply won't replicate.

But the most dismal sources of methodological introspection come from social psychology. In 2011, the field saw the publication of an article by Daryl Bem (2011) on parapsychology and psychic powers in the *Journal of Personality and Social Psychology*. Oddly, the *Journal of Parapsychology* didn't return the favor by publishing papers on personality and social psychology. In the same year, the field learned, much more seriously, that Diederik Stapel, a distinguished Dutch researcher, had forged data in dozens of papers over two decades (Carey, 2011), including many papers in the *Journal of Personality and Social Psychology*. One suspects that Stapel could have been unmasked sooner if Bem's psychics had read the journal instead of getting described in it.

Social psychologists—long known as a group sensitive about being seen as real scientists—are having a bad hair decade. But it is good for all of us in the social, behavioral, and health sciences to struggle with frizzing and split ends every now and then. The nuts and bolts of research should be more open, and changes in the culture of research will change how we write articles.

Disclosure statements in the Method section are one recent trend. Some researchers have floated suggestions for increased disclosure about the methods, such as disclosing whether the hypotheses were developed before analyzing the data (Kerr, 1998) or whether any conditions, participants, dependent measures, or experiments were omitted (Simmons, Nelson, & Simonsohn, 2011, 2012). Having to disclose all of one's measures, for example, ought to reduce selectively reporting the studies and findings that the researchers hoped to find.

Disclosure about methods is a good practice that journals should pursue, but my sense is that many of the proposals being floated work better for experimental, hypothesis-confirmation areas (like cognitive and social psychology) than nonexperimental, exploratory, and discovery-oriented areas. In large-scale longitudinal research and survey research, for example, the whole point is to generate massive data sets that researchers around the globe can mine for decades. Scholars who conduct secondary analyses of massive data sets like MIDUS (National Survey of Midlife Development in the United States) or HRS (Health and Retirement Study) could easily "omit" most of the participants and nearly all of the variables available to analyze.

The stronger alternative to disclosure is archiving the research materials online. For most studies, there's no reason why questionnaires, software files, and interview protocols can't be archived for other researchers to view. Most journals are probably reluctant to archive these files, but other institutions have created tools and space for sharing materials. For example, Open Science Framework (OSF; www.osf.io), a not-for-profit organization devoted to making science more efficient and transparent, allows researchers to create online file archives that can be shared selectively (e.g., with only a handful of collaborators) or globally. Each archive has a unique and permanent link that writers can include in their manuscript. If you're curious, you can search OSF for many of my own archives.

One step better is to archive raw data that have been stripped of potentially identifying information (Wicherts & Bakker, 2012). Widespread access to raw data would transform how research happens and how we write research articles. Data shenanigans of the Stapel sort—manufacturing raw data—would get even rarer, and researchers could more easily obtain raw data for reanalysis and meta-analysis. The availability of raw data is currently atrocious. In a case study of frustration, Wicherts, Borsboom, Kats, and Molenaar (2006) described their fruitless attempt to obtain raw data for new articles published in APA journals. After months of requests and hundreds of e-mails, they received only 26% of the data sets—despite the papers' being less than a year old and being published in journals that require adhering to APA's data sharing rules. Availability gets worse as the years pass. After requesting raw data from articles published over many years, Vines et al. (2014) found that the likelihood of obtaining a study's raw data dropped by 17% for each year that passed since an article's publication. On the basis of their findings, Vines et al. concluded that "in the long term, research data cannot be reliably preserved by individual researchers"

(p. 94). Anyone who has seen the disheveled state of faculty offices probably agrees.

The large-scale archiving of research material and raw data will make writing a Method easier in most ways. Rather than describe questionnaires, instructions, or sampling processes in tedious detail, for example, you could summarize them and point readers to an online archive of materials, either on your webpage, the journal's page, or on a resource like Open Science Framework. Appendixes in articles will probably fade away, taking their tedious equations and word lists with them. But Methods will become more work in other ways. The archives will need to be formed, double-checked, and documented, adding steps and tasks that didn't exist before.

## WRAPPING UP

Writing the Method section first, like smiling when happy and talking to babies in a high-pitched voice, appears to be a human universal. And if everyone does something, then it must be a good idea, according to research (Eidelman, Crandall, & Pattershall, 2009). Method sections are the easiest to write and the hardest to get wrong. The goal is to describe the things that your readers want to know and to convince them that your approach was apt. By connecting your research to others' research in many minor ways, you'll make the point that all good Methods must make: We did this well.

# 6

# Writing the Results

An odd idea in art criticism is that art is mostly about words (Wolfe, 1975). A museum exhibit on "Terrors and Terrariums: The Numinous Gothic Imagination in Modern Southern Painting," for example, might have two dozen paintings but 10,000 words: a set of "artist's statements" by the painters that ground their vision, didactic text placed next to the painting, a long essay by the curator that describes the selections and how they embody the exhibit's theme, and many breathy thanks to the agencies who funded the thing. A purist might feel that great art needs no explanation, but the rest of us are glad for some hints about why those box turtles have halos.

Scientists, like painters, sometimes give their audiences too much credit. Your results—the data, descriptive statistics, structural models, and inferential tests—make much less sense to your readers than you think. Many Results sections thus have the same flaw: They read like a transcription of SPSS output, a morass of numbers and tests packed into paragraph form. The Results section is where the numbers are, to be sure, and the point of quantitative research is to make a point using statistical methods. But we shouldn't hang our numbers on a wall, stark and unadorned, and hope that the critics get what we're trying to say.

In this chapter, we describe how to write a Results section that emphasizes words and numbers, discourse and digits. The Results section is where you make your case: The Introduction proposed an idea, the Method described how you tested it, and now you must justify your reasoning with evidence. Instead of dumping the stats in the Results and explaining them in the Discussion, we can use the Results section to remind readers of our ideas, describe what we found, and explain what they mean (Salovey, 2000). Our findings will thus be easier to understand and more persuasive.

## A SLEEK RESULTS SECTION

When you peer review articles for journals, you get a glimpse at what the bottom of a barrel looks like after a vigorous scraping. Papers that never see the light of print often have atrocious Results sections: They are either stuffed with statistics in no obvious order, lacking basic analyses, or both. Published Results sections are usually good enough, but many are as austere and somber as a German avant-garde theatre production. Too many writers take a grim joy in having only facts, only numbers, only hypothesis tests. As a professor, I can relate to this sort of self-denial, but it makes for confusing reading.

Our purpose in the Results section is to make a point: "This is what we found, and this is what it means." Your Results section should thus have a tight take-home message. But in writing, as in all things, simplicity is hard. Many writers feel shy about contextualizing their findings in the Results, having been warned as undergrads that "the Results is for numbers—just say what you found. Save your explanations and interpretations for the Discussion."

I would suggest the opposite: The ideal Results section would have no numbers. Such a vision is quixotic, of course, and it should remain in the realm of fantasy, comfortably nestled among "retire to New Hampshire and build boats" and "invent coffee-flavored tea." But a Results section should read well and make sense even if the numbers were stripped out. A simple way to get a compelling Results section, in fact, is to write it without the numbers, revise the text until it sounds right, and then plug in the statistics. Try it at home.

Placing as much information as possible into tables is probably the easiest way to clean a cluttered Results section (Salovey, 2000). Readers will get sleeker text as well as tables that convey more information than could be included in the text. Many kinds of statistics work well in tables: Descriptive statistics, correlations, regression weights, and summaries of model fit are common examples. To make the tables worth the space, add more information to a table than would be practical in the text. For example, a table of descriptive statistics should go beyond the usual suspects of means and standard deviations to include additional measures of central tendency (e.g., median or modal values) and variability (e.g., confidence intervals, minimum and maximum values). (As someone who has edited and reviewed more papers than my subconscious can repress, I would make a special plea for including 95% confidence intervals in your tables.) Figures, like tables, alleviate the strain on the text. Readers will understand a pattern of effects, a structural equation model, or a time series quickly if they can see it.

## STRUCTURE OF THE RESULTS

Most Results sections will have two main parts: a short boring part and a longer interesting part. The boring part is like the copyright page of a book; the interesting part is the story itself.

### Boring Details: The Copyright Page

Every fine novel has some greasy nuts and bolts holding it together. A book's copyright page isn't glamorous, although some writers do surprising things with it (e.g., Eggers, 2000), but it has essential information for the people who need to know it. (Lest you doubt, try withholding Library of Congress Cataloging-in-Publication information from a librarian and behold the ensuing woe and wrath.) And it's concise: It packs the tedious details into a short space that is easy to skim or skip.

Your Results section should do the same thing. Most research has some tedious details that can't be omitted but don't belong in the story. You have seen a lot of these dumping grounds. They appear at the start of the Results, and they usually have a heading like "Data Reduction," "Preliminary Analyses," "Model Specification," or "Analytic Plan." The nature of your analyses will determine what goes here, but Exhibit 6.1 lists some common elements. In general, any housekeeping issues that some readers will expect to see can go here. Don't worry about being boring: Say what you need to say and then get to the story.

EXHIBIT 6.1. Examples of Material for Your Results Section's Copyright Page

- How summary scores were computed, such as the glamorous details of reverse scoring, summing, and averaging
- The condensing and treatment of biological data, including software programs, algorithms, and filters
- Estimates of internal consistency, interrater reliability, or temporal stability
- Details about centering and intraclass correlations for multi-level models
- Outlier screening and detection
- Tests of whether your humble data meet statistical assumptions
- Nuts and bolts of model specification and fit statistics for confirmatory factor analyses
- Information about estimation methods—such as ordinary least squares, maximum likelihood, or Bayesian Marcov Chain Monte Carlo—and any special software used for it
- Consideration of missing data

## Core Findings: The Story

Your story is what your readers came for. What did you find? Did it work? Will the lad get the damsel in a feat of derring-do? Here's where you describe and explain your findings. If you're planning to send your paper to a new journal, you should browse a few articles to get a sense of the journal's preferences for statistics. Some journals, for example, require the reporting of effect sizes; others don't care. Some prefer standard errors; others prefer standard deviations. And a few have idiosyncratic requirements—I'm talking about you, $p_{rep}$ (Killeen, 2005), a star-crossed statistic that *Psychological Science* briefly required authors to report but is now extinct (Doros & Geier, 2005; Iverson, Lee, Zhang, & Wagenmakers, 2009; Trafimow, MacDonald, Rice, & Clason, 2010).

When discussing your main findings, you should strive for a concise and logical structure. It's hard to encapsulate every kind of Results section you might write, but a couple intuitive rhetorical principles will help. First, move from the *central to peripheral:* Present your most important findings first. Don't build up to them in a dramatic crescendo like a mystery novel. Most of your findings only make sense in light of the central findings, so you should describe the most important effects first. Second, *establish then elaborate.* Before launching into qualifiers, mediators, and moderators, establish the central point and then elaborate on it. Readers don't understand exceptions to the rules unless they first learn the rules.

128

Subheadings and paragraph breaks are effective markers of transitions in your Results section. This is the part of the paper where you will be forgiven for short and skimpy paragraphs. A paragraph with only one or two sentences feels undeveloped and awkward in an Introduction or Discussion, but it is acceptable and effective in the Results. A few short paragraphs, each devoted to making a distinct point, can be easier to understand than one long paragraph that combines them.

For a fresh, contemporary feel, you can structure your paragraphs using Johann Herbart's ideas from the 1830s about apperceptive masses (Dunkel, 1969). We saw this approach when we discussed Pre-Intros (see Chapter 5). This basic structure reminds the reader of the conceptual issue behind the analysis, describes the analysis and results, and then explains what the findings mean for the conceptual issue. This remind-describe-explain method works well. Present each analysis as a problem: State the basic issue to remind the reader of why you are doing this, report and describe the test, and then briefly explain it. Not every paragraph in your Results will or should look like this, but I encourage you to try it for your central findings: It will help your readers and reinforce your message.

## PRESSING PROBLEMS, MISCELLANEOUS MATTERS

### How Should I Report Advanced Statistics?

What do you do when your research involves statistics that most of your readers don't understand? In the halcyon days of the 1950s, everyone understood correlations, $t$ tests, and analyses of variance (ANOVAs) because that's mostly all there was, apart from the hoity-toity realm of exploratory factor analysis. In modern times, sophisticated researchers can't keep up with every development in the many frontiers of applied statistics. As a result, you might find yourself trying to publish research that most of your readers don't understand. This is a problem: You need readers to understand what you are doing, but a peer-reviewed journal article isn't the place for a comprehensive didactic overview of your analytic approach. In short, you need to explain the methods enough so that readers get it but not so thoroughly that you appear patronizing.

When writing near your field's statistical frontier, it helps to keep in mind that readers are responsible for learning new statistical tools on their own. Readers know this, and they don't blame you for their lack of training in the field. What they want from you, however, are some citations to good didactic sources (such as what you found helpful when learning the method) and a practical overview and justification of the method. If you can briefly describe the new method and explain what it buys you, readers will be happy.

Over time, these justification and description sections get shorter and then disappear. In papers from the 1980s, you'll see justifications for using newfangled regression interactions instead of the tried-and-true median splits; these days, median splits are a pox on your paper. In the 1990s, studies that used structural equation modeling (SEM) would include at least a paragraph that defined model fit, explained what the fit indices meant, and cited papers related to model fit. Today, in journals that publish a lot of SEM work, many papers simply rattle off the model fit acronyms without explanation or elaboration. By reading some recent papers that used the method—from your target journal, ideally—you can get a sense of how long your description should be.

## What About Peripheral Findings?

In Results sections, as in life, it is hard to know when to quit. A vexing writing decision is how to handle peripheral findings, those effects that aren't obviously immaterial or obviously pressing. A common Results flaw is to have a section or two of extra "because they are there" effects. Writers usually include these sections out of a misguided sense of completeness or an unwillingness to amputate their interminable master's thesis with a chainsaw. You usually find the fringe findings at the end of the Results, where they do less harm, but you'll occasionally see these at the beginning, where they are deeply confusing.

Good papers have a core message, a main point they wish to make. Your message gets diluted when peripheral findings are tossed in. It is hard to know where to draw the line of relevance, but there is one. On the one side stand effects that contribute to your message— these are findings that reviewers expect to see. On the other side is a motley miscellany of effects. Some of the findings are interesting in their own right and could be the center of a different paper, but they don't move your current argument forward.

Reporting every conceivable analysis of every last variable in the study is bad—less is more, more or less. Text gets confusing when irrelevant material is added. Readers adhere to a simple conversational logic: If you add a paragraph or two of ancillary findings, they assume that you think it is relevant. But they can't see how it is relevant, so they attribute their confusion to their own comprehension failure (bad) or to your failure to grasp the key points of your own message (worse).

If you think some analyses are peripheral to your argument but worth adding—perhaps a subset of readers would want to see them, or perhaps you're feeling compulsive—there are two good ways to go about it. The first way is to point out to the reader that the material is peripheral, which will make its relevance to the paper's main purpose easier to discern. You could start the section, for example, with something like, "Although [main idea] was the focus of the research, interesting secondary effects appeared for [secondary idea]." The second way is to locate the extra material where it won't interrupt the flow of your otherwise tight Results section: A footnote is an excellent place for a paragraph of exploratory or secondary analyses.

## What About a Combined Results and Discussion?

In your many travels through the pages of our journals, you have probably encountered the "Results and Discussion" section. What is this curious beast, and should you bring one home with you? This section combines, obviously, the Results and the Discussion into a single section that presents and interprets the findings in light of the ideas advanced in the Introduction. These combined sections are excellent in two contexts. When you have a brief paper, like a short report or comment, you can save space by presenting and discussing the findings in the same place. And when you have a multistudy paper, you can combine each study's Results with its poststudy Discussion—this affords smooth shifts from one study to the next. The combined Results and Discussion is optional—reviewers and editors rarely demand it—but it's an effective trick for sleeker papers.

## What If My Study Only Partly Worked?

Reviewers prefer airbrushed perfection, but most papers have a few freckles and scars. How should you write up the Results for a study that didn't completely work? You should first consider whether the flaws are fatal and whether the paper is worth your time in light of your lengthy writing to-do list. Null effects and spurious effects can be persuasive in some contexts, such as when researchers scanned a dead salmon to show that fMRI research can yield a lot of false positives (Bennett, Baird, Miller, & Wolford, 2010). But not every study is worth publishing—some fish are just dead.

In most cases, though, the flaws are minor and the scars are small. When seeking to write up inconsistent or unexpected findings, accept that you probably won't get your paper into a top journal. Such places have their pick of the litter, and your runty manuscript won't get picked. You could still get into a good journal, but be realistic. When developing the manuscript, be open about what you did and found. Reviewers have an eerie eighth sense for contradictory findings. Beginning writers commonly try to obscure flaws, hoping people won't notice, but the reviewers always notice the problem and then eviscerate the authors for trying to hide something. You needn't belabor your problems in a fit of self-mortification, but be candid.

At some point, however, you might have to pull the plug. If your half-worked study is rejected from most of the journals on most of the world's continents, the flaws are probably bigger than you thought. Some studies are informative—readers learn something of value despite the blemishes—so they ought to be published. But others are simply flawed—readers gain only confusion, so your paper sucked knowledge out of the world. Remember that we're writing for impact, not for mere publication. If you want to publish your study because of sunk costs, not because it offers something of value to your peers, you should probably let the data die gracefully.

## Wrapping Up

Most of us think of the Results section as where the numbers go. That's true, but they shouldn't go there unsupervised lest anarchic riots of $p$ values and

ANOVAs ensue. The Results section should have more and less quantitative information than the usual paper: much more in the tables and figures, and less in the text. By shunting the digits into tables and figures and by wrapping them in words that position and explain them, your Results section will be as lean and self-sufficient as a grizzled survivalist.

# 7

## Writing the Discussion

All good things must come to an end, but most boring things are interminable. Your research article, whether good or boring, has to end sometime, and the last stop, the station at the end of the line, is the Discussion. Readers and reviewers enter the Discussion with informed opinions about your work, so the wrap-up rarely changes anyone's mind. But we aspire to writing excellence, if only out of authorial pride or professorial perfectionism, so we want to write a great Discussion instead of a mediocre one.

Most research articles, like most high school dating relationships, end awkwardly. This chapter thus gives strategies for crafting a strong Discussion. As your paper's final section, the Discussion is your last chance to reinforce your message and emphasize your strengths. When done well, a Discussion wraps up your research, points to some interesting connections and implications, and waves farewell to the valiant readers who took the time to read your entire paper.

## What Makes a Discussion Good?

The purposes of the Intro, Method, and Results sections are obvious: They sell your ideas, describe what you did, and reveal what you found and what it means. But what do Discussions do? What does a good one accomplish? A Discussion has two goals. The noble goal is to build connections with ongoing theories, debates, and problems. In this sense, we shouldn't *discuss* anything per se in the Discussion—we should integrate ideas, forge links, build bridges. By hooking your findings into your field's important problems, you illuminate the significance of your work.

The ignoble goal is to warehouse the nuts and bolts that don't fit elsewhere. Modern Discussions are like ministorage units, a place to stuff the unloved furniture that is too ugly for the house. The Discussion offers a place to respond to reviewers' criticisms, to tackle awkward partial replications and unsupported predictions, to discuss things you find boring but the reviewers want to see, and to consider limitations of the work. These fiberglass lampshades and particleboard bookcases have to go somewhere.

In all cases, a good Discussion has two qualities. First, it's particular and specific, not generic. Too many Discussion parts look lifted from other papers. When discussing limitations, for instance, people often discuss limitations that apply to vast swaths of scholarship, not to their particular study. When discussing implications, people often mention vague, generic implications that could follow from dozens of similar studies, not their own specifically. Generic elements make a Discussion seem aimless and bland.

Second, a good Discussion focuses on the strengths of the research, not the weaknesses. All work has weaknesses, to be sure, but some Discussions are like long lamentations where people belabor their minor failings and cower before the criticisms raised by reviewers. If you think your work has deep flaws, don't publish it. Otherwise, be candid about your findings while focusing on the strengths that motivated you to do the research and want to share it with your peers. Someone should leave your paper with the sense that the work was important, that it has implications for things the field cares about. Be sure, then, that your positive take-home message—the one idea you want your readers to get—doesn't get lost in a thicket of ascetic self-recrimination.

Discussions follow a tacit template. APA Style doesn't dictate that these elements should appear in this order, but social norms have evolved to provide a structure that most articles use. Violating social norms leads to ostracism and legwarmers, if 1980s high school movies are to be believed, so don't do it—follow the herd. You'll recognize the template from articles that you've read: Exhibit 7.1 describes the parts. The template sounds simple enough, but of course nothing is too simple to evade our obsessive approach to strategic writing. After sketching out the parts, we'll consider how to write a Discussion for the ages, or at least the ages old enough to vote.

EXHIBIT 7.1. A Template for the Discussion Section

**Required Elements**
- Recap: In one to three paragraphs, review the animating ideas from your introduction and summarize what you found.
- Connect: Link your ideas and findings to important ongoing problems.
- Resolve: Face up to any awkward findings or unexpected results, handling them as well as you can.

**Optional Elements**
- Limitations: Briefly note limitations to your methods, with an emphasis on your work's strengths.
- Future Directions: Vaguely note one or two research directions implied by your findings.
- Implications for Practice: Describe how people working in the trenches can put your findings into action.
- Conclusion: Write a brief paragraph that summarizes the project's central ideas and findings.

A Discussion has two components. The first consists of the required parts that will appear in all your papers. The Discussion begins with a recap, a brief summary of your paper's animating ideas and major findings. The recap is followed by a handful of connections, perhaps two to four ways that your research links to and informs other ideas. If necessary, your Discussion then resolves dangling issues, such as comments raised by reviewers, alternative explanations, or quirky findings.

The second component consists of mix-and-match optional parts: A few papers might have all of these, most will have some, and a few will have none. The parts include describing limitations of your work, spelling out directions for future research, considering implications for applied workers and practitioners, and summarizing the big beast of a paper in a single vainglorious paragraph. These parts are optional depending on the journal—yet another reason to pick your journal before writing your paper (see Chapter 1). For some journals, essentially every article they publish has a section on limitations: Only the swift and hardheaded will submit a manuscript without that section. For many basic science journals, however, discussing limitations and practical implications is uncommon. Consult your target journal and follow the flock.

## THE REQUIRED PARTS

### Recap

The recap, the start of the Discussion, reintroduces the paper's purpose and guiding ideas. After the storm of methods and statistics, your readers will appreciate a reminder of why anyone should care and what it all means. Great recaps are an art. In one to three paragraphs, they summarize the paper's animating ideas, describe the central findings, and show how the results delivered on the promises made in the Introduction. When done right, they are a self-contained snapshot of the entire article—you can read them alone and get the gist of the research. Exhibit 7.2 presents two recaps from recent articles. Each one starts globally, much like the Pre-Intro that opens a paper (see Chapter 4), and then funnels toward the find-

The first recap paragraph from Ladinig and Schellenberg (2012):

> Different people listen to different types of music, which motivated our exploration about whether this variation is associated with individual differences in the way music is experienced in the first place. One possibility is that listeners in general tend to like music that makes them feel a certain way (e.g., happy), although the most effective music in this regard could vary across listeners. Another possibility is that individuals vary according to which emotional response determines how much they like a particular piece. Our results provided support for both perspectives. (pp. 150–151)

The first recap paragraph from DeWall et al. (2011):

> People in exclusive romantic relationships, by definition, have one partner. Yet, alternatives to one's relationship partner are ubiquitous. People in relationships often express little to no interest in those alternatives and derogate those alternatives (Johnson & Rusbult, 1989). Psychological commitment to one's partner helps make this resistance possible. Therefore, people with a dispositionally avoidant attachment style, who feel uncomfortable having closeness and commitment in their relationships, should be especially likely to express interest in alternatives and to engage in infidelity. (p. 1313)

ings. Like long abstracts, these recaps hold up well on their own. Having not read the articles and knowing nothing of the Method and Results, you nevertheless find the project convincing.

You might be tempted to skip the recap, thinking, "The Intro was only a few pages ago—readers will remember. I'll just jump right into a soul-baring exegesis of my study's limitations." No, they won't remember—omitting a recap is the path to abject madness. Methods and Results sections make readers myopic by forcing them to wade through pages of methodological and statistical minutiae. When they stumble out of the Results, confused and blinking from the sunlight, you must reorient them to the purpose of your work and remind them of why they waded through those pages in the first place.

## Connect

After your recap, you should draw connections between your work and other important theories, findings, and problems. Research is influential when it has something to say about problems that your colleagues care about. You might hope that your readers would discern these implications on their own, but most of them won't. No one is closer to your work than you, so readers expect you to tell them why your work matters.

Depending on the length of your paper and the norms of the target journal, you should pick two to four connective issues. You needn't make an intricate web like a conspiracy theorist pinning newspaper clippings with yarn and thumbtacks—just find the handful of important connections, the things other researchers will care about. If you're stuck and unsure what to say, think of your research more abstractly. There aren't many kinds of thematic implications—Exhibit 7.3 lists the big ones, and reading through that list will spark some ideas. Research should change minds and bring about new beliefs. What do you want readers to believe after reading your paper?

Headings contain the sprawl in a Discussion, and the start of the connections section is a good place to put one. You can have a single heading that covers everything or separate headings for each connection— just see what works.

---

EXHIBIT 7.3. A Taxonomy of Implications

Viewed globally, research can have implications for . . .

- *theory:* What do the findings mean for the field's major theories?
- *how something works:* Does the paper change our understanding of processes, dynamics, and mechanisms?
- *why or when something happens:* Can we better predict when something will occur or gain more insight into its causes?
- *what something is:* Has our sense of the phenomenon or construct changed? Does it seem simpler or more complex, or more like or unlike something else?
- *how research should happen:* Should we test, study, assess, manipulate, or sample differently as a result of the research?
- *claims made in other published papers:* Can you speak to an interesting conclusion made by other researchers?
- *things that happen in the scary and overrated real world:* Do the findings say something incisive about social justice, human health, teaching and learning, the legal system, social relationships, or anything else we face daily?

---

**Resolve**

Most research projects studies have a few pimples and scars: Not everything works the way you hope. Research ought to have a few beauty marks—if anything, probability theory and power analysis make pristine projects seem slightly suspicious (Schimmack, 2012)—but you'll have to expose them to the scrutiny of your audience. In your final required section, you confront and resolve any awkward issues that need to be handled. The natural place is after discussing connections, but this isn't a hard-and-fast rule.

What kinds of problems get resolved? Viewed abstractly, there are two kinds. First, sometimes unexpected research problems must be resolved. One or more results may have been contrary to your predictions, to other findings in the research, or to established findings in the literature. Some unexpected and unpleasant surprises are methodological: Some measures or procedures may have gone awry, such as when an established measure flops, sampling goals go unmet, or a manipulation fizzles. Second, sometimes reviewers raise issues—either problems or differences of opinion—that must be resolved. The range of such bickering is infinite.

Like other animals, researchers can flee to the safety of the flock when in trouble. Most problems can be handled by pointing to published studies that found similar things. For example, you probably aren't the only one who didn't find an established effect or who had a well-known method or measure fail flamboyantly. For other problems, future research is the great resolver—you can sketch out the kind of work needed to settle the issues at hand.

If you're aware of problems, get in front of them—don't make the reviewers ask you to discuss them. As we've said before, no one fools anyone in this business. For convincing an intelligent and informed audience, candor and evidence carry the day. Sweeping your flaws under the bed never works: A couple reviewers live under there, after all, with the dust mites and the forgotten stuffed penguin. Make your best-reasoned case, using arguments and published work, about why things aren't as bleak as they seem. At the same time, don't go on and on about it. Readers use length as a cue to importance, so spending most of your Discussion bemoaning your flaws and foibles sends the wrong message.

## THE AWKWARD OPTIONAL ELEMENTS

### Limitations

The most nefarious part of the Discussion is the section on limitations. This section is as optional as bow ties and patent leather shoes, but most authors feel obligated to slap some limitations into everything they write. If most of the papers in your target journal have a section on limitations, or if your paper must adhere to guidelines like the CONSORT standards, then you must include this section. But if not, consider omitting it.

What's so wrong with discussing limitations? One problem, in my opinion, is that routinely tossing in limitations, regardless of whether there are any, violates the ideal of being specific and particular. Most limitations sections are generic: They could apply to most papers in their field. For example, most papers in cognitive psychology and social psychology use young adults enrolled in the university as participants, and this usually gets raised as a limitation. Regardless of whether this counts as a flaw, a limitation generic to a field of science is rarely worth mentioning. Ditto for using self-report measures and cross-sectional designs: The world of psychological science understands their strengths and weaknesses. Exhibit 7.4 captures the spirit of the typical generic and uninformative limitations section—you'll recognize most of it from dozens of other papers.

But the biggest problem with routinely slapping in a paragraph of limitations is that most papers in good journals have no limitations. The researchers didn't do, measure, test, or sample everything under the sun, but they did what they did well. All projects have boundaries and emphases, what George Kelly (1955) called a *focus of convenience*. Staying focused, doing one thing well, and keeping it tight are not limitations. It is both baffling and sad to read tremendous papers that describe namby-pamby limitations after presenting an intricate and difficult research project that took many years, many people, and many millions in National Institutes of Health funding to execute.

I admit that my attitudes are unorthodox. Most researchers are happy to crank out a few generic limitations, so there's pleasure to be had in ritual self-flagellation. But I think routinely trotting out limitations

EXHIBIT 7.4. Limitations, Limitations, Everywhere
Limitations

Here's a limitations section I'd like to see someday—it hits all
the right notes:

> The present research has several limitations worth noting.
> First, the sample was restricted to people living in the
> United States. It is possible that the nature of the constructs
> and processes under investigation would be different for
> other groups, so the findings should be generalized with
> caution. Second, we employed only self-report, peer report,
> psychophysiological, and functional neuroimaging as mea-
> sures. It is possible that measures from other domains—such
> as psychoimmunology, polysomnography, and experience
> sampling—would reveal different effects. Third, the present
> work was cross-sectional and thus cannot demonstrate cau-
> sality. Longitudinal work is thus needed: Most longitudinal
> designs also cannot demonstrate causality per se, but we feel
> obligated to suggest it because our study is cross-sectional,
> which is stigmatized in some circles.

> Finally, readers interested in examining the present
> hypotheses should be aware that it is possible that the
> study could turn out differently if conducted by different
> researchers with different samples and different measures at
> a different year on a different patch of the planet. Because
> different is scary and same is comforting, researchers should
> be afraid to follow up on our research. Indeed, theoretical
> physical cosmology suggests an infinite number of parallel
> universes, and it is possible that the findings are not sta-
> tistically significant in all of them. Until the results are in
> from those parallel universes, the present results should be
> viewed with considerable caution.

for every paper sends the wrong message about how we view our science. Research should move us past the zero point, defined by common sense and ignorance (Atkinson, 1964). If failing to measure every possible thing on every possible subgroup is a limitation, then we are tacitly evaluating research in terms of how far it falls short of perfect knowledge, not how successfully it moves us out of ignorance. The first approach tries to create knowledge; the second tries to avoid uncertainty. Avoiding uncertainty is an ignoble aim for science. Most studies move our knowledge forward—we are less ignorant than we used to be—but no study illuminates everything we could hope to know. Science is a candle in the darkness (Sagan, 1995), and while some candles are brighter than others, there's no shame in seeing only a few feet in front of you.

With that said, you will often be required—by a journal's norms, an editor's request, or real problems—to include a section on limitations. How can you write a good one? First, unless something went horribly awry with your research, you can keep this section short: One paragraph is perfect for palliating the overactive consciences of anxious reviewers. Second, keep it relevant: Omit features generic to your field of research unless they happen to be real problems for your particular study. And third, keep it focused on your strengths: Limitations are merely future directions under a different, guilt-ridden name. Your research didn't do everything, but it did some things well. You can remind readers of this in your limitations section. For example, you can point out, if necessary, that starting where you started is sensible and should give researchers the confidence to extend it to new samples, domains, and contexts. Try this at home. When even your limitations section tacitly conveys the merits of your work, then you've mastered the craft of writing for impact.

## Future Directions

Beware the siren song of future directions. Unless your target journal wants to see this section, omit it. Your Discussion should emphasize your work's strengths, and the worst way to do this is to compare your dowdy project to a sexy one that you'll probably never do. Reviewers can fall under the spell of this alluring phantom study and write, "The authors should conduct that study and include it in a revised version of this paper." I have seen this sad tale unfold many times as an editor and reviewer.

There are good times and places for describing future studies. If one implication of your work is that it opens up some intriguing new problems, you can sketch out some directions for future work in the connections section. Giving other researchers guidance on how to follow up your study will increase the impact of your paper. If you have some thorny issues and prickly reviewers to handle, your resolving section should describe the kinds of studies that would handle them. But dance with the one who brought you—keep the strengths of your study in mind. Future work can fix problems, but it also can expand on strengths.

## Implications for Practice

Some papers must have a section that describes practical implications: what the research means for teaching, learning, human health, social justice, or any other practical way that it can be applied in the real world, which you can recognize by its relative lack of books. Many papers shouldn't have this section, and that's fine: Science should have both basic and translational work in its portfolio.

Discussing practical implications is surprisingly tricky. If practical implications are fundamental to your work—perhaps you studied methods for training therapists, teaching idioms to nonnative speakers, or reducing weight gain among newlyweds—then this section should go after the recap. You want to front-load your big ideas and big implications, so your connections section is essentially your practical implications section. The impact of your paper will largely depend on readers coming to believe that your work is effective and worth a try, so sell it.

Many papers, however, are more persuasive when they omit practical implications. A good Discussion, if you recall, should be particular—it should be unique to a project. Your paper turns flabby and namby-pamby when it peddles generic, off-the-shelf implications that apply to dozens of papers and that are too diffuse to be useful. Readers tune out; you lose credibility. For example, basic clinical psychology papers might include a half-hearted paragraph on possible implications for treatment, basic cognitive psychology papers might speculate on implications for teaching and learning, and basic developmental psychology papers might give some moribund implications for early childhood education. Readers in these fields have seen these paragraphs dozens of times. They undercut the important implications and slow the momentum of the Discussion.

Don't say anything if you don't have anything unique and insightful to say. Some work is basic—implications for practice, if any, are far down the road, way out where it turns to gravel and gets blocked by cows. Reviewers and editors at basic science journals will not reject your paper solely because it lacks a practical implications section, so there's little risk to omitting it.

## Summary

Like the ending credits to a movie, a summary informs the audience that the drama is over and they should take a minute to get their emotions under control before reentering reality. These sections are a single paragraph, usually preceded by a heading like "Conclusion," "Summary and Conclusion," or "Concluding Thoughts." Summaries, like cat ownership, solar panels, and Paleo diets, evoke surprising acrimony. Some writers never add them; other writers always add them and hound the abstainers to do so when they serve as editors and reviewers. As someone who owns half a cat, my attitude is more ecumenical: I include a summary when a paper is long, when an editor or reviewer suggests adding it, or when I can think of a clever way to end. But for most short papers, I think you can simply stop, pivot, and walk off stage.

If you include a summary, you have two options. The basic option gives a snapshot of the project, much like a tiny abstract. In one paragraph, describe the major ideas, findings, or implications. As with abstracts (see Chapter 8), you should close the paragraph with an affirmative statement—end on a line that points out something good about the work. Exhibit 7.5 gives an example of a basic summary in its natural habitat (Hoggard, Byrd, & Sellers, 2012). Notice how its ends. Hoggard et al. (2012) did a fine job with this summary: It becomes increasingly general and ends with reasons why the authors' ideas and research questions matter. The last paragraph thus sends readers on their way with a pitch for the work's significance.

The deluxe option is to develop a quirky summary, a snapshot of the work that introduces a new idea, implication, or example. The goal of a quirky summary is to end with a bang, or at least a smile. Some articles, for example, close a circle opened in the Pre-Intro (see Chapter 4) by revisiting an anecdote that introduced the paper. Other articles end with the authors applying the findings to themselves, raising a new comical or interesting example, or simply writing an elegant turn of phrase.

EXHIBIT 7.5. Waving Goodbye: Basic
and Quirky Summaries

**Basic Summaries**

From Hoggard, Byrd, and Sellers (2012):

> In conclusion, although African American college students
> may appraise racially stressful and nonracially stressful events
> similarly when other situational characteristics are taken into
> account, they use very different coping strategies in response
> to the events. This finding suggests that there may be some
> utility in racial coping models (e.g., Scott, 2004; Utsey et al.,
> 2000). Regardless of whether African Americans' responses
> to racially stressful events is best conceptualized within a
> generalized stress and coping framework or a framework
> specifically focused on racial stress, it is imperative that
> such a focus recognizes that "coping" is occurring. African
> Americans are not passive victims with respect to the racial
> and nonracial stressors that they experience. Rather, they
> take active, effortful action both to alleviate the situation as
> well as to manage the emotional consequences of the event.
> These effortful coping actions may be the key to understand-
> ing the increased health, education, and legal risk that African
> Americans face as a result of exposure to racial stressors as well
> as a potential source of resilience and survival. (pp. 337, 338)

From Greengross, Martin, and Miller (2012):

> Overall, the results of this study suggest that professional
> stand-up comedians are a distinct vocational group: they
> score higher on all humor styles, on humor ability (as revealed
> by their rated cartoon captions), and on verbal intelligence
> than college students, but they also show different patterns of
> correlations between Big Five personality traits and humor

*(continued)*

154

EXHIBIT 7.5. Waving Goodbye: Basic
and Quirky Summaries (*continued*)

styles, and a discrepancy between on-stage persona and private personality. Comedians' professional success depends not just on their short-term spontaneous humor production ability, but also on their long-term skill, dedication, and ambition in crafting and refining an effective act that can be modulated for different audiences in different cities with different tastes, traits, backgrounds, and levels of inebriation. It also depends upon their fluent, strategic use of affiliative humor and self-deprecating humor when interacting with club patrons, club owners, booking agents, and other comedians. Apart from our quantitative results, we were impressed by the range of personality traits, social skills, and intelligence required to succeed in the stand-up comedy business, and by the potential fruitfulness of stand-up comedians as a group for further research in personality, humor, and creativity. (p. 80)

**A Quirky Summary**

From Risen and Gilovich (2008):

The studies presented here document a widespread belief that it is bad luck to tempt fate, even among those who would deny the existence of fate. So what happens when people believe things they know are false? They do their class reading, bring their umbrellas, hold onto their lottery tickets, and (try to) avoid boasting or presuming anything too soon. And when they don't follow their intuition, they think about how they might be punished. All the while, they shake their heads and roll their eyes, knowing that their behavior and worries are unwarranted. (p. 305)

# Wrapping Up

We have reached the end; all your text is done. If you feel the urge for wistful reminiscence, you can read what you wrote: an Intro that sells the idea, a Method and Results that explain what you did and found, and now a Discussion that reinforces your message and highlights its relevance for important problems. I have found that people respond to finishing a big burly paper with different feelings. Some people have a Skinnerian postreinforcement pause and descend into lazy inertia, others feel exhilarated relief, and more than a few have a melancholic crisis of meaning. But before you put on the flip-flops and stop shaving, remember that you still have some arcana to get together: references, tables, figures, and a title and abstract. And by now you surely know that we have more to say than should ever be said about that stuff—Chapter 8, our darkest chapter, awaits.

# 8

## Arcana and Miscellany:
## From Titles to Footnotes

When people talk about writing up some data, they have the beefy parts in mind—the Introduction, Method, Results, and Discussion. Everything else is trimmings— the fat of references, the cartilage of figures, the gristle of abstracts and titles. A paper feels done when it's all over but the arcana, but some of the most important parts remain unwritten. We're close to the end of this book, and I would understand if you were tempted to skip this chapter. Who wants to read about the glories of references? Is there anything to say about footnotes, and if so, were humans meant to possess such dangerous knowledge?

The manuscript elements in this chapter are admittedly less glamorous than the Introduction and less intricate than the Results, but they aren't less important. All pieces of a paper play a part in impact. Some elements, like titles and abstracts, grab and hold your readers; other elements, like references, figures, tables, and footnotes, build your credibility and position your work. Everything in a paper, from the noble Introduction to the humble footnotes, conveys your skill, professionalism, and obsessive perfectionism. So once again, for the final time, we venture into the breach.

## REFERENCES

Getting tested on APA Style for references and citations is a grim rite of passage for psychology majors, and for many of us, that's the last time we put serious thought into what our references should look like. But references serve two key functions, and most papers get only one right. The mundane function is to document your ideas so readers can follow your intellectual trail (Hyland, 2001). Nearly all papers do this well. The rhetorical function, in contrast, is to situate your work, to convey how you view your ideas and which audience you are trying to reach.

The rhetorical function of references is underappreciated, and it is easy to understand by comparing cases when it goes well and awry. Consider a paper that explores memory biases related to emotional material in a depressed sample. Such a paper could speak to different audiences: Researchers interested in memory, in cognition and emotion, and in clinical psychology, for example, could be primary audiences, so the work could be couched in different literatures. The good strategy is to (a) cite work from the journal to which the paper will be submitted, (b) include many papers from the domain within the past 3 years, and (c) cite papers that people in that domain see as important and cite often themselves. The references will thus be substantially different depending on the journal—and hence the audience—that the paper is pointed at. The bad strategy, in contrast, is to (a) fail to cite work from the journal and from the domain, (b) include mostly old papers, and (c) cite eccentric stuff that the authors happened to read and felt like citing (see Exhibit 8.1 for some examples).

EXHIBIT 8.1. Reasons for Including a Reference

Here's a motley miscellany of reasons for including a reference. Some are crafty, some are scurrilous, and some are funny.

- *Seeding the clouds for desired reviewers*. It's true: Most editors will consult your References section when making a list of possible reviewers. You can seed the clouds by citing people who you think won't maul your paper with a hatchet.
- *Attracting specific readers to your paper*. Because impact is measured in part by citations, researchers pay attention to who is citing their work. If you want to make specific people aware of your research, cite them in your paper—they'll probably notice. This sounds vain, but an easy way to keep track of what's happening in your area is to see who is citing certain papers, and sometimes those papers are yours.
- *Boosting the impact factor of a journal you publish in*. For journals that don't publish many papers annually, an extra 10 citations a year to recent papers will noticeably improve its impact factor. Impact factors, which are taken too seriously when researchers and departments are evaluated, can be hacked if

*(continued)*

EXHIBIT 8.1.  Reasons for Including a Reference *(continued)*

researchers excessively cite papers from the journals they publish in, thus making the journal seem more influential than it probably is.

- *Recovering sunk costs.* You made it through a long book or dense article, exhausted but proud. With all that pain invested in reading it, by Jove, you're going to cite it.

- *Waving hello to an obscure journal.* Some journal titles sound made up, the product of a grad-student drinking game gone horribly right. But no, such journals are merely obscure. Our childish side delights in waving hello to such journals, and the reference is a fun Easter egg for the readers who notice.

---

You might scoff, thinking, "Scoff! No one makes those mistakes," but editors and reviewers see them all the time. It's common to see manuscripts that fail to cite anything from the past 3 years. A stale reference list makes reviewers suspect—correctly, I think—that the manuscript has been kicked around the journals for a few years, receiving only minor tweaking after each rejection. A surprising number of papers fail to cite much from the domain. I often review manuscripts submitted to creativity journals, for example, that fail to cite anything published in any creativity journal. They might cite work published in cognitive, educational, and business journals relevant to creativity, but they ignore the work published in outlets that have creativity scientists as the core audience. This never ends well. The reviewers and editors feel slighted, and the authors look like oblivious interlopers.

References should thus be curated, not listed. Of all the things you could cite, cite the papers that both document and convince. Documentation isn't enough—note that the poor strategy still documents how the authors developed their ideas, but it fails to tacitly convey that the paper is linked to the concerns of the audience. If anything, it conveys that the authors haven't read enough work by the audience they are trying to reach. Most studies can be pitched to different audiences, and the papers you discuss and cite are how you do that. By picking your journal ahead of time (Chapter 1), you have already given thought about how to couch your work, so this will be easy for reflective writers who plan ahead.

Finally, I shouldn't have to say this, but don't cite what you haven't read. If you can't give a solid synopsis of what a paper did and found, you haven't earned that reference yet. Apart from professional pride and self-respect, citing only what you've read prevents reviewer wrath. Because editors pick some reviewers by looking at your references, you're likely to get the authors of papers you didn't read as reviewers. Those reviewers will sniff out your ignorance with the humorless tenacity of cadaver dogs. Remember our dictum: You will never fool anyone, especially the authors of papers you pretended to read.

## Can There Be Too Many?

I snicker when my undergraduate students ask, "How many references do we need to have?" Ah, the callow concerns of youth. As we mature, our citations expand with our waistlines, and more than a few of us have morbidly obese reference lists. Some time back, Reis and Stiller (1992) showed that the number of references in one leading journal had increased 300% over a few decades. More recently, Adair and Vohra (2003) sampled a broader number of journals and expressed alarm at the trend toward massive reference lists. There's no question that the reference lists in old papers seem scrawny—a few seem almost anorexic. The zenith is surely a paper by Brehm and Cole (1966), which is famous both for its clever ideas and for its lack of references—it cites nothing.

It is natural to pine for the older days, when most cars had three pedals and DDT kept the bedbugs away, but there are reasons why few people buy vintage cars and old mattresses. There are few incentives for having few references and, as we described earlier, many incentives for having a lot. Your references position your work, convey your sensibility as a researcher, and connect readers to your work. Unless the journal imposes a limit, don't worry about having too many references.

## Is Citing Yourself Unseemly?

What about citing yourself? Most people are comfortable in the skin of their published work; others, though, feel dirty after citing themselves. Regardless of modesty, self-citation is rampant. Roughly 10% to 20% of all citations are self-citations (Fowler & Aksnes, 2007; Hyland, 2001), depending on the discipline and the author. Brysbaert and Smyth (2011) criticized this self-absorbed state of affairs. Researchers, they claimed, self-cite "not because the self-citations are necessary to understand the argument . . . but because they are good for the researchers' esteem, by means of self-enhancement and self-promotion" (pp. 134, 135). (I'll leave it to you to check if they cited themselves.)

I think there's more to self-citation than ego stroking. In the sciences, most people work in specialized subfields. When you're an active researcher, much of the recent work published in your subfield is your own. And we aspire to a cumulative science, both for the field as a whole and for our own research careers (see Chapter 10). If you aren't citing your own work, then what you're writing doesn't build on your prior ideas— it sprawls outward instead of growing upward (Ring, 1967). Finally, one should never discount laziness, that venerable mainspring of human action. We know our own work best, so it comes to mind easily when we need a citation.

Beyond the practical reasons why self-citation is inevitable, there are good rhetorical reasons to cite your work. Hyland (2001) argued that talking about one's own work builds disciplinarity and authority. By citing your published work, you tacitly convey, "I'm part of this scholarly conversation and I've done this before." As we noted when discussing the Method (see Chapter 5), citing your past work that used similar procedures is a powerful way to put reviewers' minds at ease and to link your work to the established body of methods.

But what about impact, our big theme? It turns out that self-citation, like most crimes, pays well if you stick with it. Analyses of citations have found that each self-citation has a cumulative 10-year payoff of around 3.7 citations from others (Fowler & Aksnes, 2007). The reasons seem complex, but the big ones are probably authority and visibility. Your readers do similar research themselves, and if they took the time to read one of your papers they will want to know what else you've published in the area. Self-citation describes what you've done and saves readers time tracking down your other papers. So don't be bashful about citing your own work. Of the many things we could denounce in this world, rampant self-citation seems low on the list.

## TITLES

Your manuscript's title is like a carnival barker, luring and wheedling people inside the dark tent of your research. The title is where most readers will get grabbed, either reluctantly or willingly, into learning more about your work. In older times, researchers would choose simple descriptive titles along the lines of "The Effects of This on That" or "Stuff, Something, and Whatever." In a world with only a handful of journals, each of which appeared quarterly in one's mailbox, such sparing and monastic prose wouldn't hurt you. But in modern times, when most subfields have a dozen important journals, many of which appear monthly, you need to work harder to snatch your readers.

A good title should be inviting and relevant. In a fun book that invited distinguished social psychologists to discuss their turkeys—articles they thought were important but had little impact (Arkin, 2011)—more than a few researchers rued their choice of titles. When discussing his most underappreciated work (Cooper & Jones, 1969), Cooper (2011) assigned some blame to a bland title that failed to excite readers' interest: "What you call your research tells interested but over-burdened readers whether they should read your article or move on. The moment is soon lost. If readers' eyes do not stop at our entry in the table of contents, they may never look back" (p. 180). Batson (2011), too, thought that his most unloved article (Batson, 1975) received little attention because of a poor title. In his case, the title lacked some critical keywords that caused authors of review articles to overlook it. Readers who mined the review articles for references thus never found it, creating a vicious cycle of obscurity. He rec-ommended that writers "talk in categories in play in the field, using terminology and titles that pigeonhole you properly" (p. 211).

To grab readers, we should consider how they encounter our titles. These days, people are plugging keywords into a database, browsing lists of recent articles on a journal's webpage, or reading a journal's table of contents in print or online. In all cases, people are implicitly looking for keywords that match their research interests, so your title should have slots for at least two keywords. Don't go for hip synonyms or literary allusions—get your staid and boring key terms in there. Batson's (2011) advice is wise: Couch your work in the terms favored by the community of researchers. People searching databases are usually searching via keywords; people scanning a list of in-press papers will stop at a title with relevant terms.

Once you have the keywords down, you can decide what tone you want for your title. Some titles are straight and somber; others are silly, intriguing, snarky, combative, or confusing. Pick whatever tone matches your text. It is okay to play it straight: You needn't be cute or sassy. Psychology is in a slightly silly phase with its titles, but much like the phase in which little kids like to induce dizziness by spinning around, it will pass. Be as somber and formal as you like—you'll have to live with your title for the rest of your career. For my papers, I shift the title's tone on the basis of the target journal. Some fields, like biological psychology and clinical psychology, tend to have staid and formal titles; other fields, like the psychology of art and creativity, are open to fun and zany titles.

The title's structure is your other big decision. You have a lot of options; research on the titles of scientific papers reveals surprising variability in the forms titles take (Soler, 2007). The colon title—with a main title, a colon, and a subtitle—is popular and versatile. Such titles are more striking when the main title and subtitle vary in length: The shorter part will grab attention and ring in the mind. Some researchers rebel against subtitles, and that's fine so long as the title conveys the substance of your work and contains conventional keywords. An underappreciated option is to use questions, either as the full title or as one of the elements. Questions have an inherent grab, and they highlight your paper's animating question.

Titles pose a few traps. First, a phrase or reference might be too topical. It is tempting to snatch an idea from current news or popular culture—they will grab a reader's interest—but your paper, if you're lucky, will be read years and years from now, perhaps by your initial readers' grandkids. Are you certain that future readers will get the reference? And if they do, will it still seem cool? Recall, when uncertain, what you liked, listened to, and wore in high school—times change. Second, your title might be too obscure: If readers don't get your reference, your title will seem confusing. I fell into this trap with one of my first papers (Silvia, 2001). The main title came from a line in an obscure Günther Grass novel I was reading, and no one ever got it. Finally, avoid special typographical characters: subscripts, superscripts, mathematical characters, and the like. How well will these render in databases that get searched with various browsers and devices? Can you trust your readers to dutifully type them in when they cite your paper?

A good title is a tricky thing to pull off, but don't over-overthink it—sexy titles won't compensate for homely research. Cooper (2011) said it best: "What's in a title? In the short term it may make a difference, but it in the long term it is overwhelmed by the substance of your work" (p. 180).

## ABSTRACTS

Your abstract, for several reasons, should be one of the last things you write. Writing a concise overview of your work is painful, and it is human nature to defer painful things to the brighter future. And it's hard to summarize your work when you don't know what you'll say. But whenever you get to it, take the time to craft a good abstract. Most of your audience will read only your title; many more, if interested, will then read the abstract. Few people will then go on to read the whole article, so your abstract needs to be both informative and compelling, a research paper in miniature.

In the deep past of the 1990s, most journals had the same length requirements for abstracts. This was a blessing: After adjudicating on the thousands of writing's small choices, you don't want to decide whether the abstract should be 120, 150, or 250 words. In the anything-goes modern era, a new licentiousness has afflicted journals: Some want 120, some want 150, others want a beastly 250; the *Publication Manual of the American Psychological Association* (APA, 2010) doesn't take sides, noting simply that most journals prefer abstracts between 150 and 250 words. This cannot stand. You might not care, but recall our strategy of picking backup target journals with similar format guidelines. It is annoying to write a 250-word abstract for one journal, chop to it 120 for another, and then expand it to 150 for a third.

A good abstract accomplishes two things. First, it attracts database searches with keywords and their synonyms so that your paper pops up when it should. You need to cram all the relevant search terms and keywords into your abstract, even if the abstract's style suffers somewhat. Reaching for synonyms to avoid repetition is usually tacky (Zinsser, 2006), but such tackiness is okay in your abstract. Don't be shy—sometimes a synonym is the difference between attention and obscurity.

Second, a good abstract provides a persuasive snapshot of your work's main ideas, methods, findings, and implications. The hardest part of writing a persuasive abstract is expressing the animating idea, the significant element in your work, but you can do it. One strategy for doing so is to bookend the abstract with assertive and interesting sentences. For your first sentence, aim for something with grab. Questions and global assertions work as well for abstracts as they do for Intros (see Chapter 4), and many writers find that the first line of the Intro is a smashing first line for the abstract. After conveying what you did and found, end with a good sentence that provides an affirmative statement or conclusion. Don't end with "Implications for stuff and whatever are discussed." That sounds fussy and Victorian. End with a statement about what your work means—state the implications concisely. Your last line will stick with the reader and reinforce the importance of your work.

## FIGURES AND TABLES

Make a lot of figures and tables. When talking about your Results (Chapter 6), we argued that figures and tables allow you to streamline your text, which makes your paper more readable, and to expand the amount of data you report, which makes your paper more open and informative. You'll occasionally find a journal that limits the number of figures and tables, but most don't. If you want to avoid writing, you could productively procrastinate by reading some books about figures and tables (Few, 2012; Nicol & Pexman, 2010a, 2010b). They will give you some inspiration and make your papers better.

## FOOTNOTES

Footnotes, like politics, religion, and semicolons, should not be debated in polite company. On the one end are the denouncers who are quick with their standard attack: "If it's worth saying, it's should go in the main text!" On the other hand are the teeming hordes of scholars in the humanities, for whom a life without footnotes is not worth living. In the social and behavioral sciences, footnotes are allowed—it's okay to have them, and it's okay to omit them, so follow your conscience on this one. I like footnotes because they serve some useful functions. Footnotes allow you to dig into some nitty-gritty details without hurting the coherence of the main text. Some information is important to only some readers, and a footnote takes those readers aside without disturbing the rest. Footnotes also segregate tangential ideas that reviewers wanted to hear about but don't fit well elsewhere.

I offer two cautions with footnotes, however. Don't use them to circumvent page limits and word limits. That doesn't fool anyone, and you'll have to slink away with your triaged manuscript to another journal. And don't go all humanities on everyone, footnoting every peripheral thought, interesting aside, and quirky conjecture that came to mind while typing. (I have long suspected that the urge to footnote is correlated with the urge to italicize words for emphasis and start sentences with "Well" and "You see"—someone should do a study on that.) Your article, on so many levels, isn't a David Foster Wallace novel. Aim for no more than one footnote per three or four manuscript pages.

## APPENDICES AND SUPPLEMENTAL MATERIAL

We are entering the gilded age of appendices. In the print era, one would occasionally see an Appendix tacked on to a paper—a list of words used in a cognitive experiment, the items for a new self-report scale, or some greasy details best separated from the genteel Method—but it was uncommon. Journals didn't save page space with appendices, so anything worth saying got said in the paper's main sections. The Internet, however, has stepped forward to serve its true purpose: as a repository for obscure stuff that, despite our vain hopes, no one will ever read. Many top-notch journals shunt extensive information into online supplements, and many researchers archive research materials and data themselves. The printed article can thus hit the high points and refer readers to the online material, which is many times longer. Like kids cleaning their rooms, researchers can cram the lumpy and unsightly clutter into the closet.

As we discussed in Chapter 5, an intriguing trend is the posting of raw data as supplementary material. A sign of the times is an editorial published in *Intelligence* by Wicherts and Bakker (2012). In a surprisingly lively piece, they argued that researchers can boost a paper's impact by publishing the raw data along with the article. The raw data will attract the interest of tinkerers, grad students, meta-analysts, and assorted scientific rubberneckers. By posting the data and inviting people to publish new analyses, you will bring more attention and citations to your work. As the methods of meta-analysis evolve from analyzing descriptive statistics to modeling raw data, researchers will increasingly want your data files.

Posting data files as supplementary material is an emerging practice, so a few kinks need to be worked out. The biggest ones concern de-identification. It's obvious that names, phone numbers, and addresses would be omitted, but it's harder than one might think. If information in the data can be paired with other available information, many cases can be re-identified. In some cases, some combinations of scores might be so uncommon that an informed observer could infer someone's identity (e.g., a small college might have only one freshman female who would list her nationality as Nigerian). Researchers should consult federal guidance for de-identification and data sharing before making data publicly available (e.g., U.S. Department of Health and Human Services, 2012). If you're uncomfortable posting data into an online archive or appending it to an article, you can simply invite people to e-mail you for a copy.

## RUNNING HEADS

Running heads used to be a bigger deal back in the days when people would get a journal in the mail, adjust their pince-nez, and thumb through the pages. The authors' names, printed *verso*, and the running head, printed *recto*, would grab the attention of readers browsing through the printed issue, indicating that they should stop flipping pages and summon their manservant for their inkwell and parchment. Journals still print hardcopies, and running heads are still required, but they are less functional than before. APA Style describes the running head as an "abbreviated title" (*Publication Manual of the American Psychological Association*, 2010, p. 229) that is no more than 50 characters long, so your running head will have around the same number of characters as a Tolstoy short story.

What can one do with a running head? How can we overthink this humble manuscript element? Your first (and best) option is to say something short—no one will notice, so our limited time on Earth is probably best spent on other writing decisions. Simply condense your title and move on to other things. The second (and snarkiest) option is to say something clever—no one will notice, so a running head is a sly spot for wordplay and unexpected humor.

## Wrapping Up

I never understood people who say, "Don't sweat the small stuff"—either they suffer from anhidrosis or they own only gargantuan things. How you handle small details reveals much to your readers about your commitment to the craft of science writing and your obsessive nature, two things that are probably highly correlated. But with the small stuff suitably sweated, your paper is done. Our next chapter thus describes how to submit your paper to a journal and deal with the reviews, tasks known to make beginners perspire.

# III

## PUBLISHING YOUR WRITING

# 9

## Dealing With Journals: Submitting, Resubmitting, and Reviewing

Much of the world's most interesting writing is self-published. Each new technology, from papyrus to the photocopier, has allowed anyone with an intriguing idea and a free weekend to reach some readers. But much of the world's worst writing is self-published, too, so readers should thank the editors and publishers who toil in obscurity to curate the written word. Some writers never grow out of seeing editors and publishers as barriers to reaching their audience. Before denouncing the gatekeepers and going our own way, however, we should remember that most of our readers live inside the gates, where life is civilized and the books are good. Unless you like camping alongside writers who leave copies of their agitprop tracts and vampire-romance novellas outside your tent, it's time to learn about the System, the Process, the Program, and how to get with it.

This chapter discusses journals: how they work and how to work with them. Dealing with editors, reviewers, and publishers, the gatekeepers of peer-reviewed science, can intimidate newcomers to scientific publishing, but the system for polishing bumpy manuscripts into peer-reviewed gems is fairly straightforward. The chapter starts with how to submit papers to journals, an intuitive process that is hard to bungle. The core of the chapter, however, is devoted to dealing with the reviews, revising your paper, and resubmitting it, an obscure process that is easy to bungle. You get publications by resubmitting good revisions to journals, not by sending them your first versions. The fragile moment of resubmission is where things can turn glorious or tragic—as I've learned from my own mistakes, from reviewing hundreds of papers, and from serving as an editor. As we'll see, a strong revision is part offense and part defense: There are simple and sound principles that will boost your odds. The chapter ends with some thoughts on reviewing articles for journals, an essential service to the field and an obligation of published writers.

## Submitting Your Manuscript

Submitting a manuscript is easy. Because you picked the journal early, crafted the paper for its audience, and wrote for impact, your paper will be shiny and sparkly and ready for the world, like a debutante at the world's geekiest cotillion ball. Most journals make it easy to submit an article. A typical journal has a web portal that allows you to fill in some forms, upload your files, and then click submit. In some cases, the system creates a PDF proof for you to approve—be sure to check this file for mistakes in the special characters (e.g., mathematical and statistical symbols, superscripts, formulas), tables, and figures. A few technology holdouts ask authors to e-mail the manuscript to the journal editor, who then grumbles about how hard it is to find his inkwell by the erratic light of the whale blubber lamp. To be charitable, I'm old enough to recall the sepia-toned days when I would march to the photocopier, make five copies, and then fret about whether I could find a postal envelope large enough to fit everything—good times, good times. Before submitting the paper, reread the submission guidelines to be sure that your paper meets the journal's length and format requirements.

In addition to your manuscript, most journals want a brief cover letter. These letters are generic and straightforward. Exhibit 9.1 provides a template for you to use. The first paragraph lists the title and provides some standard declarations: The research was approved by your IRB, it hasn't been previously published, and it isn't under review elsewhere. If journals want additional declarations—the author guidelines will point them out—you can dump them at the end of the first paragraph. The second paragraph is optional: It's a chance to suggest reviewers and an action editor. If the journal has published similar work—and it

EXHIBIT 9.1. A Template Submission Letter

[Date]

Dr. [Editor's Name]

*[Journal Name]*

Dear Dr. [Name]:

We would like to submit the attached manuscript, "[Appealing Title of Your Paper]," for consideration in *[Journal Name]*. The paper has # words of text (# total), # tables, and # figures. The research was approved by our institution's IRB, it hasn't been previously published, and it isn't under review elsewhere.

This paper [brief, one-sentence snapshot of paper]. If you are seeking suggestions for reviewers, several researchers (list two to four names) have published related papers recently in *[Journal Name]* and would thus be good options. *If relevant:* [Associate Editor's Name] has published extensively in this area and would thus be particularly well suited to serve as the action editor.

With all the best,

[Author names]

[Corresponding author's postal address, phone and fax numbers, and e-mail address]

---

probably has, if you chose the journal strategically—you can point out a few friendly faces who published similar papers. (Naturally, you cited those people in your paper.) And if the journal has many editors and you think one is particularly qualified, you can point that out, too.

In the spirit of overthinking the small stuff, I would offer two tips for submitting your paper. First, listen to the nagging voice in your head that says, "Maybe I should read this through one more time." Apart from the inherent virtue in obeying voices heard in one's head, you'll probably find a few typos and missing references to fix. Second, don't let your manuscript ripen. Some writers let a finished paper sit for a week or more until they feel some vague sense of readiness. The few days you take to feel ready are days that reviewers could spend avoiding your article—let them do your procrastination for you. As any debutante will tell you, don't hesitate when you make your entrance.

## UNDERSTANDING DECISION LETTERS

Your manuscript's coming out party, however, comes to a crashing end once you get the editor's action letter. An action letter has a couple parts. The first part is the editor's own remarks, which convey the editorial decision; the second part has the reviewers' comments. Only a few outcomes can happen: Your paper will be accepted, your paper will get rejected, or you will be offered a chance to revise and resubmit. Let's unpack these three.

### Accept

An acceptance is hard to misinterpret: The editor writes that your paper has been accepted and reminds you to fill out some publication forms. You shout "Yay!

181

It's manicotti time!" and make untoward and perplexing gesticulations that your office mates later realize were intended as dancing. It's a myth, by the way, that editors never accept a first submission outright. I have had a few papers accepted flat-out with no changes, and as an editor I have accepted a couple papers essentially as-is. It happens more often than you would think, which is one more reason why the "Let's just get the paper out and wrap up the small stuff when we resubmit it" attitude is misguided.

### Reject

The confusion about editorial decisions happens with revise-and-resubmit and reject decisions. Some editors use the word *reject* in two ways: to mean what speakers of the world's 70 English-speaking nations mean by *reject* (as in "I never want to see that wretched document again") or to mean *revise and resubmit* (as in "I'm rejecting this draft but am willing to consider a revised version"). So, bizarrely, the appearance of the word *reject* doesn't mean that your paper is rejected. What you must look for is language that conveys a willingness to consider a revised draft. If the editor is willing to see it again, then it is a revise-and-resubmit decision. To make this concrete, Exhibit 9.2 provides some examples of revise-and-resubmit language and rejection language from my own deep pile of rejection letters.

The journal's web-based journal management portal may be easier to interpret than the editor's own letter. If

EXHIBIT 9.2. Examples of Revise-and-Resubmit
and Rejection Decisions

---

**Revise and Resubmit**

- I have now heard back from two reviewers whose comments
  are shown below; as you can see, both of them liked this contribution and thought that it was appropriate for publication
  in [Journal Name]. However, they do suggest a few very minor
  changes. If you make these to my satisfaction we will be happy
  to publish the paper: It will not need to go out for review again.

- Reviewers have now commented on your paper. You will see
  that they are advising that you revise your manuscript. If you
  are prepared to undertake the work required, I would be pleased
  to reconsider my decision. . . . The reviewers have raised a
  number of issues that you should address. If you are able to
  address these issues and explain what you did in the cover
  letter, no additional review may be necessary.

- On the basis of the reviewers' recommendations and my own
  reading of your manuscript, I cannot accept this manuscript
  for publication in [Journal Name] at this time. However, if
  you believe that you can address weaknesses identified in the
  reviews, you are invited to revise and resubmit your manuscript
  to [Journal Name]. I must emphasize, however, that there is
  no guarantee that a revised manuscript will be accepted for
  publication.

- Your manuscript has now been reviewed and elicited rather
  positive reactions in the reviewers, who respectively asked for
  a major and minor revision. My own reaction to your manuscript was rather positive as well, although I had a major concern in addition to the comments and suggestions provided
  by the reviewers. My first inclination was to reject this manuscript. However, I have decided to give you the opportunity
  to resubmit a major revision of it. If you feel convinced that

---

*(continued)*

183

you can successfully address the issues below, then I would
be happy to consider a revision of this ms, which may or may
not be sent out for further review. Alternatively, it may be
that you feel highly uncertain about the success of such revision, in which case I would like to encourage you to resubmit
this research to another outlet. In any case, I wish you good
luck as you prepare a revision of this manuscript, either for
resubmission to [*Journal Name*] or to another journal.

**Reject**

■ Both reviewers have concerns that prevent them from supporting publication of the manuscript, and my own reading of your
paper places me in general agreement with their evaluations.
I am sorry to report that I will not be able to accept your paper
for publication in [*Journal Name*].

■ I have received comments from three experts; their comments
appear below. On the basis of their comments and my own
independent reading of your manuscript, I am sorry to inform
you that I have decided to decline your submission for publication in [*Journal Name*].

■ Although your work has many strengths, it does not appear to
be a good fit for [*Journal Name*]. I must therefore reject your
submission.

you log in to the system and look at your paper, you'll
probably see a label for the decision, such as Accept,
Accept Pending Minor Changes, Revise and Resubmit,
and Reject. If you are still uncertain about what the
editor was trying to tell you, don't be shy about sending
a follow-up e-mail.

Despite your most creative attempts at hermeneutics, you will often conclude from an editor's letter that your paper was rejected—sometimes with the fanfare of a scapegoat being driven out of a plagued village. Rejections are easy to act on. You have only two choices. The first is to dump your paper in a metaphorical file drawer; the second is to submit it to a different journal. Many beginners, discouraged from their first peer-reviewed thumping, feel like taking their ball back and going home. There are surely some occasions when a paper deserves the file drawer—the research might have fatal flaws that the reviewers graciously pointed out—but your default choice should be to send it somewhere else. If you thought through your research before conducting it—deciding whether it was worth your time and considering the kind of journal in which it would get published—you won't have a lot of turkeys.

Submitting your paper to a new journal is basically like the first time you submitted it. If you followed the advice on picking journals (see Chapter 1)—plan for one or two backup journals in case your first choice rejects it—you probably already know where to send your paper. Before sending it out again, make any changes that seem worthwhile. A set of reviews is free writing advice from scholars in your field (Lambert, 2013): Be constructive about the feedback. Reviewers usually have a lot of good ideas, and you shouldn't let peevishness interfere with improving your work. If you need to be scared straight, there's a good chance that one of the prior reviewers will be a reviewer again. Subfields of knowledge are small, and editors use similar tactics for picking reviewers, so reviewers commonly get called to serve for many versions of the same paper. Don't incur their wrath by ignoring their feedback.

I'm often asked about dealing with rejection— both the anticipatory fear that keeps people from submitting and the postreview despair that makes people want to quit. When I bought my first car, I vowed never to complain about gas prices—I chose to drive, after all. When you choose to submit manuscripts to journals, you will get rejected, and you should vow to avoid complaining about it. I view rejections as a sales tax on publications: Rejections are a relatively constant proportion of submissions, so submitting a lot means getting rejected a lot. As a result, there's nothing unusual, personal, or atypical about rejection for writers to "deal with": Learn from the reviews, revise it, and send it somewhere else. The sun didn't burn out, your cat still loves you, your house is still standing.

I disagree, then, with the old advice that researchers should put their reviews in a metaphorical drawer for a few days: "Read them when you have more emotional distance," I once heard. Some people need to get over themselves. If you submit 10 papers a year and wait a few days to act on reviews, you have lost 30 days, a full month of the year, in the service of bubble wrapping your fragile sensibilities. It is easy for me to say this, having been rejected perhaps 200 times by journals, publishers, and funding agencies—my own publishing emotions are at a distance visible only to an infrared deep-space telescope—but publishing your ideas for scrutiny by the world's scientists isn't for snowflakes. When you get reviews, read them immediately and act on them within 2 days.

One action you should avoid, however, is protesting to the editor who rejected your work. Over the years, you'll get rejections that strike you as unfair—reviewers might misunderstand your paper, lack the competence to review your work, or use the paper as a whetstone for their axe—and you'll be tempted to write to the editor and defend your work with the righteous zeal of a student interning at a hip nonprofit. Occasionally I hear of someone who has had some success with such protests: Some editors are willing to reconsider a decision and get new reviews on a paper. But I never do it, and I strongly discourage you from doing it, too.

There's a thin line between your perceptions of a rejection as unfair and a mere injury to one's pride: How sure are you that a gross injustice has occurred? Submitting articles is probabilistic. Sometimes the large element of chance hurts you, but sometimes it helps you: You'll occasionally get reviewers who had a good day. It evens out. Regardless, editors don't want to hear from you. They have a big stash of manuscripts that need action letters, and you risk their wrath by bringing up old business. The author guidelines for the journal *Personality and Individual Differences* say it best: "Correspondence regarding decisions reached by the editorial committee is not encouraged."

## Revise and Resubmit

Rejections and acceptances have straightforward behavioral consequences: revising and submitting elsewhere (rejections) and the unseemly manicotti dance (acceptances). Revise-and-resubmit decisions, however, are more complicated. Revise-and-resubmit decisions fall on a continuum of encouragement. On the one end, editors say that the changes are relatively minor and they anticipate acting quickly on the revision without seeking additional reviews. On the other end, editors say that the changes would be extensive, that they would seek additional reviews, and that they're uncertain if the paper's problems can be handled. Exhibit 9.2 shows examples of decisions along this spectrum.

Your default choice should be to revise the paper and send it back, regardless of the level of encouragement. As a writer, I view *revise and resubmit* as *conditionally accept*; as an editor, I only invited a revision when I expected a revised draft to be accepted. To understand why, you need to crawl into the shadowy mind of a journal editor. Editors do not feel reluctant about rejecting your paper. Most papers get rejected, so the life of an editor is a stream of rejecting manuscripts and occasionally inviting someone to resubmit. Editors will not coquettishly lead you on because they feel guilty about rejecting you—if they say they'll consider a revision, they mean it. If anything, editors would rather reject you so they can cull the implacable and ceaseless backlog of manuscripts that need rejecting, but they saw merit in your work and are willing to see it again.

That is why your default choice should be to do the tedious work needed to revise and resubmit. It will occasionally be rational to send the paper to another journal instead of revising it, but this is rare—perhaps 10% of the time. The editor and reviewers might want changes that you're unwilling to do—they might be expensive, beyond your skills, or harmful to the paper's integrity and potential impact—so you'll occasionally take your ball back and go home. But again, be wary of letting wounded pride and the slog of revising tempt you into submitting the paper elsewhere.

## How to Revise

There's only one way to revise a paper: quickly. Most papers get rejected, so you have beaten the odds. The editor saw some promise in your humble manuscript, so you should get the new and improved version back in front of him or her as soon as you can—strike while enthusiasm is high and the paper's appeal is fresh. As an editor, I appreciated rapid resubmissions. They took less time to read and process because I didn't have to dredge up the old reviews and notes. A fast resubmission is also a mark of a committed researcher with good writing habits. In these days of online journal portals, most revisions have a deadline—usually 2 or 3 months—before the link to resubmit the paper vanishes. People with poor writing habits skate close to the edge and occasionally fall over.

## Revising the Manuscript

Revisions are where the game is won or lost. Most researchers win, but a few collapse like an inebriated shot putter. Through inexperience, irascibility, or ineptitude, writers can mess up even the easiest resubmission. Lest you doubt, Exhibit 9.3 lists some examples that I've

EXHIBIT 9.3. When Resubmissions Careen Off the Rails

- An editor suggested that three small tables with the same format should be combined into one table, thus saving page space and typesetting expense. Inexplicably, the authors refused, so the editor, in a second decision letter, made the suggestion more forcefully. The authors refused to combine the tables a second time.
- For some small percentage of authors, reviews puncture their fragile ego and unleash a fit of narcissistic rage. Nothing makes an editor want to break out the red inkpad and *REJECT* stamp like a long ranting letter that excoriates the reviewers and stubbornly defends the paper against their nefarious criticism.
- Two reviewers pointed out that a statistical composite had been formed incorrectly and that a few effects seemed quirky. In the revision letter, the authors noted that in rechecking the statistics they found widespread errors in the raw data file that explained the quirky findings, and they assured the editor and reviewers that the new version was pristine. The editor lost faith in the data and the researchers' competence and rejected the paper.
- Editors often ask writers to trim a manuscript, sometimes substantially. For one paper, an editor suggested deleting a third of the material. The authors, perhaps confused about fractions, resubmitted a draft that was a third longer.

seen as a reviewer and editor. To avoid such calamities, you need a constructive attitude. Being constructive doesn't mean caving to a reviewer's every offhand suggestion or compromising the integrity of your ideas; it means dealing with the reviews in good faith, being open to making major changes to your manuscript, and presuming that the peer-review process makes most papers better.

Now that we're feeling full of goodwill, where should we start? The first step is to get the editorial letter and go through it, line by line, to identify *action items*, comments that require a decision on your part and a response in your resubmission letter. Some of the editorial letter, you'll find, is filler material that requires no action, such as the boilerplate elements of the editor's letter, prefatory comments by the reviewers, food-for-thought ideas, and miscellaneous discursive discourses. But most of the letter consists of suggestions for ways to change the paper: things to add, to delete, to reword, to rethink, to reanalyze. For my papers, I print out the letter, underline each comment that requires action, and then make a note about how to handle it. And there are only three options: You can change, resist, or punt.

## Changing

Most of the comments will involve changing your paper. Most changes are minor: expanding the detail in your

Method and Results, clarifying ambiguous statements, adding references, or deleting a few paragraphs. But some are major, such as recasting the conceptual basis for the research, adding new data, or converting a long manuscript into a short report using only a rusty machete and steely resolve. Either way, the peer-review process leads to a lot of changes. This irked me when I got started, before I developed the tough skin of a leatherback sea turtle, but my experience writing, editing, and reviewing has shown me that papers get much better from the process of peer review. Nearly all of my own papers improved, many vastly so, so making changes is part of writing for impact.

But what if you don't know which change to make? Editors and reviewers conflict—it happens all the time. One will want you to drop half the tables; another will suggest adding two tables, a figure, and an online appendix. One will want a discursive digression on technical marginalia; another will want you to fire up the chainsaw. If the editor conflicts with a reviewer, go with the editor's suggestion, for obvious reasons. If reviewers conflict with each other, pick a side and make your case in your resubmission letter. For vexing conflicts, it's okay to send a quick e-mail to the editor: Include the paper's manuscript number and title, briefly summarize the issue, and ask if he or she has a sense of which would be the better direction. If you're a beginner and blanch at the idea, perhaps from a fear of appearing uncertain or timid, take heart in knowing that writers do this all the time.

## Resisting

Being sober of mind and constructive in spirit, you'll make a lot of changes to your manuscript. But not every comment made by every reviewer was meant to be: A few ideas are weird, incomprehensible, self-serving, or dangerous to today's impressionable youth. Your second option is thus to resist. Naturally, you will want to resist in a constructive and collegial way—in revisions, as in political conflicts, nonviolent resistance is the most effective form (Chenoweth & Stephan, 2011).

Reviewers might think that their every comment deserves attention, but editors don't expect abject obeisance. So long as you have good reasons for resisting, it's fine. Editors find some of the reviewers' ideas weird and ill-conceived, too, so there's a good chance that the editor favors resisting over changing. But you have to have a good argument—you can't just say that you disagree. You'll need to discuss why you didn't make the changes and show that you put some thought into it.

## Punting

Your final option is punting—putting the decision in the hands of the editor. With some reviews, you're stuck between a rock, a hard place, a pokey place, and a questionably damp and sticky place. When you're stuck, you can punt a decision to the editor. Punting is best done rarely: Reserve it for when the problem is relatively minor and you suspect that the editor doesn't care much one way or the other. For example, a reviewer might suggest adding several tables that seem of little value, extensive analyses on a speculative and peripheral aspect of the research, or discussing some minor implication or connection, and the editor, in his or her remarks, didn't express a preference. If you're not sure whether to change or resist, you can resist the change but note in your letter that you were uncertain, concluding with "but we could easily add [reviewer's quixotic and parlous suggestion] if you think it would improve the paper's impact." If the issue is important, e-mail the editor ahead of time to seek guidance on the changes—don't punt the big stuff.

## Crafting the Resubmission Letter

When you resubmit a paper to a journal, you have to include a letter that describes the changes. Editors read this resubmission letter to see what changes you made and to evaluate your reasoning for suggestions you resisted. Your letter is probably more important than your revised manuscript. A good letter can seal the deal; a poor letter can lead to another round of reviews or an ignominious rejection. Failing to grasp the importance of the resubmission letter, beginning writers send something skimpy, obscure, and full of typos. Experienced writers, in contrast, give these letters their best effort.

These letters can get long. To bring this down to earth, Exhibit 9.4 lists some examples of letters I wrote for revisions that were accepted. I picked a paper from

EXHIBIT 9.4. How Long Might a Revision Letter Be?

- Silvia (2012): 10,032 word manuscript, 654 word letter (7%)
- Nusbaum & Silvia (2011): 8,546 word manuscript, 1,639 word letter (19%)
- Silvia (2010): 4,773 word manuscript, 1,246 word letter (26%)
- Silvia, Nusbaum, Berg, Martin, & O'Connor (2009): 3,919 word manuscript, 1,325 word letter (34%)
- Silvia et al. (2008): 15,653 word manuscript, 2,488 word letter (16%)
- Silvia & Brown (2007): 5,486 word manuscript, 832 word letter (15%)
- Turner & Silvia (2006): 4,340 word manuscript, 2,953 word letter (68%)
- Silvia (2005): 11,673 word manuscript, 2,578 word letter (22%)
- Silvia & Phillips (2004): 6,596 word manuscript, 786 word letter (12%)
- Silvia (2003): 5,659 word manuscript, 720 word letter (13%)
- Silvia (2002): 8,917 word manuscript, 2,010 word letter (23%)
- Silvia & Gendolla (2001): 18,988 word manuscript, 3,168 word letter (17%)

each year between 2001 and 2012 and went back to see how long the letters were. Exhibit 9.4 lists the word counts for the manuscript (all inclusive) and for the letter (also all inclusive). The letters vary in absolute and relative length: It is common to see letters over 2,000 and 3,000 words, which is longer than some papers. For many of my revisions, it takes me longer to craft the resubmission letter than to make the changes in the manuscript.

The tone of your resubmission letter should be guided by two themes: *constructive* and *responsive*. This should be your stance, your sound. Don't be huffy, snippy, angry, self-righteous, or condescending. Seriously. The editor doesn't care about your feelings—or even about your paper that much, given that most journals get more good work than they can publish—and you'll look like a narcissistic fool for picking fights with anonymous people who volunteered their time to comment on your manuscript. Likewise, don't be fawning and flattering. The editor doesn't think the reviewers are a bunch of geniuses whose every word should be carved in gilt-edged tablets and ritually buried in a Mithraeum, and neither do you, I suspect—but if you happen to be going to a Mithraeum anyway, please bury a copy of this book.

Just as I disagree with letting reviews sit for a cooling-off period, I disagree with the common advice to write the angry letter you feel like writing, let it sit while you gain some distance, and then revise it to remove the self-righteous denouncements of the reviewers. Beyond wasting time that should be spent working through your writing backlog, this behavior reinforces the counterproductive mind-set that publishing your work is an adversarial process that deserves your anger.

Now that we have our plays-well-with-others hats on, how do you write one of these letters? The letter starts with boilerplate material: the date, the name of the editor and the journal, and the manuscript's number and title. The main part, and the hard part, is the body of the letter. There are two ways to structure the body of the letter: by reviewer or by topic. Structuring by reviewer involves addressing the editor's comments and then each reviewer's comments in order; structuring by topic involves discerning the major comments across the reviews and discussing the changes in order of importance. Organizing by reviewer is much more natural for journal articles. It's easier for editors—the structure of your letter parallels the structure of their action letter—and essentially everyone does it this way. (As an aside, resubmission letters for grant proposals are best structured by topic. Such letters have tight page limits—only one page for National Institutes of Health proposals, for example—so a thematic approach is more compelling.)

The body of the letter is a grim march through the valley of arcana and marginalia. I use headings for the editor and for each reviewer, such as *Your Comments*, *Reviewer 1's Comments*, and *Reviewer 2's Comments*. Under each heading, go through the action items in the order in which they appeared in the editorial letter. Bulleted or numbered lists are convenient. For each change, briefly describe the issue and then describe the changes you made. When possible, note the page number of the revised text in the manuscript; some authors copy and paste the revised text into the letter itself, which is convenient for the editor.

You'll need to spend more time on comments you resisted than on changes you made, and here is where you'll need your constructive and responsive tone the most. As with changes, start by recapping the issue. Then discuss what you did in response to it, if anything—additional analyses, reading new literature, consulting with colleagues—and then explain why you ultimately decided not to make the change. If it helps you make your case and show that you engaged seriously with the suggestion, you can include in the letter new analyses, references, tables or figures, statistical syntax, and other elements.

## What Next?

It's possible that your revision will get rejected—it happens sometimes, and it is what it is—but it is much more likely to be accepted than rejected. You might have another round of revisions, especially if the editor sent the revision out for new reviews, but you might have your revised draft accepted outright. Getting a paper accepted, like most of life's cheery milestones, requires filling out some forms. The editor or production staff will ask you to complete some paperwork. There's always some kind of copyright transfer agreement—this gives the journal the right to publish and distribute it, as well as many other rights—and there are occasionally others, such as attesting that the research was conducted according to ethical best practices. Fill these out immediately. Most journals have a convenient online system for their production forms; others use the tried-and-true postal method.

You'll eventually get page proofs from the journal—scour those like a lasagna pan. Being young and lacking confidence in your English skills, you might believe that the professionals know what they're up to and that you'll find only minor errors. But page proofs, like diaper pails and frat-house carpets, are never truly clean. There are always grievous and bizarre mistakes. In one of my papers, the word *aesthetic* had been replaced with the archaic British *esthetic* throughout. I gently pointed out to the production person that, ahem ahem, the journal title was *Psychology of Aesthetics, Creativity, and the Arts*—spelled with an A—and it was sponsored by Society for the Psychology of Aesthetics, Creativity, and the Arts (also known as APA Division 10 and as "the division with glamorous scarves and tattoos"). The production editor corrected the spelling in my article but not in the issue's other articles—egad.

Exhibit 9.5 lists the most common errors that pop up in page proofs. You'll want to read everything—and I mean everything, from the Author Note to the table notes—as carefully as you can bear, but the things in Exhibit 9.5 are the most common errors. In addition, page proofs usually have author queries, which are questions the production team has for you. The most common query is whether an in-press citation can be updated. Page proofs are the most time-sensitive task in scientific writing. Publishers usually need these back within 48 hours, and you should aspire to 24 hours at most.

EXHIBIT 9.5. Page-Proof Hot Spots

- Special characters, Greek letters, statistical symbols, and diacritical marks often render poorly or get replaced by a weird ASCI smiley face.
- Tables are often keyed by hand, so the numbers are sometimes wrong.
- The values in tables are often inconsistently aligned (e.g., aligned at the decimal point at one spot but at the first digit at another).
- The paper's headings are frequently shifted to the wrong level: A first-level heading might be shifted to the second level and vice versa.
- Hyphens, en dashes, and em dashes often get converted into each other.
- Double-check the authors' names, addresses, and order.
- There are usually a few garden-variety typos, grammar errors, and spaces missing between words and paragraphs.
- Figures might appear fuzzy because of insufficient resolution. If necessary, you can send a higher quality file to the production team.
- Zealous, fundamentalist copyeditors might uncontract every last contraction in your manuscript, sense and sound be damned.

## OTHER PEOPLE'S PAPERS: REVIEWING MANUSCRIPTS

Once you have been around the block a few times, editors will set on you like brigands and drag you into the block's unsightly alleys—reviewing manuscripts. Unless you have served as an editor, you have no idea how hard it can be to get reviewers for a paper. To make matters more vexing, some reviewers take a perverse pride in taking forever to get around to the paper. Many people have told me that they wait until they receive an automated reminder, which is usually 4 to 8 weeks after they agreed to review. A few candidly added that they were deliberately slow to avoid being asked to review again.

People who rarely review and who are deliberately slow, I have found, are usually the same people who whine like newborns when journals take a long time to act on their own papers. The process of peer review requires peers to review, so anyone who submits papers to journals is obligated to review manuscripts. Reviewing for journals is a classic tragedy of the commons. Everyone wants to publish papers, but few want to review. As a result, the review process is too slow and too fragile.

Reviewing manuscripts should be reasonably progressive—the more you submit, the more you should review. If you're curious, in a typical recent year I have done 50 to 70 reviews for journals; served on a couple National Institutes of Health proposal review panels; reviewed a handful of grant proposals from foreign countries; and evaluated a few book proposals, edited-book chapters, or manuscripts for publishers. And this is a light load compared with what many of my colleagues do and relative to how much I submit, so I'm not griping.

When you agree to review a manuscript, you should aspire to get it done within a week. Being quick has its virtues. First, as with many tedious tasks, it's easier to do it quickly than to have it sit as an undone goal, picking at your brain and mocking you from your mental back burner. Second, editors notice and appreciate your effort. Every editor has an informal list of top-shelf reviewers who write good reviews reasonably quickly. When it's time to invite people to serve on the journal's editorial board or to serve as an associate editor, names come from these lists. You might see this as an example of no good deed going unpunished—conscientious reviewing leads to more reviewing—but you should see it as becoming embedded in your field's scientific institutions and as doing your fair share. Finally, reviewing is a good opportunity to convey your discernment, professionalism, and community-spiritedness to editors who will judge your papers.

Reviewing papers is easy. Beginners tend to be intimidated or insecure and thus write massive catalogs of every minor fault. Apart from being creepy and obsessive, like double-blind stalking, such lengthy reviews are a poor use of the reviewer's time and ungainly for editors and authors to work with. When writing a review, you should focus on the big things: Is this work important? Will it have an impact in its area? Is it a good fit for the journal? Did the Introduction write checks that the Method and Results couldn't cash? Are there serious flaws in conception, methods, or analysis? Line editing—going through a text line by line, remarking on every minor quirk—isn't required. You can point out typos, missing references, and quirks of style and grammar if you have the time and inclination, but your main goal is to focus on the bigger scientific issues.

When reviewing others' papers, remember the Golden Rule: Thrash not people with halibuts that you yourself do not wish to be thrashed with. Over the years, you will get your share of turkeys to review, but set the snark gun to neutral. Nothing is gained by condescension or mockery, and my superstitious side hopes that there is a publishing karma that rewards volunteering constructive criticism to hapless authors. Save your anonymous jeering and scoffing for the Internet—that's what it's there for.

## CONCLUSION

It is tragic when misfortune befalls good papers because their authors couldn't navigate the publication process. Editors and reviewers, for better or worse, are the gatekeepers and taste makers for your field. To get your work published, you have to send your absolutely best first draft and then engage in the revision process constructively and professionally, no matter how unnatural it might feel. But if preschool teachers can keep their cool in the daily maelstrom of shrieking and finger painting, you can be constructive and responsive when a few colleagues send you anonymous comments on your work. And with that said, I'm happy that this chapter is finished—it's manicotti time!

# 10

## One of Many: Building a Body of Work

One of the many ways that science is like pop music is the prevalence of one-hit wonders, youngsters who come out of nowhere, publish something striking, and then haunt fringe venues, like regional conferences and county fairs, for the next few decades. How can we avoid this? One of the many hard truths about academic publishing is that one paper, even if excellent, rarely makes a splash. It usually takes a line of work, a program of connected papers, a "network of enterprise" (Gruber, 1989) to get attention and change minds. Not every paper we write will be a hit, of course, but no one goes into science to publish only one notable thing. Like pop stars, researchers should seek to develop a substantial *oeuvre*, although I'm sure being huge in Finland has its comforts.

This chapter thus takes the long view of academic writing. How can we develop a program of research and bring attention to it? What isn't worth writing? And how will we get all this writing done?

## One Is the Loneliest Number

Impact comes from a line of work, a series of linked papers on the same topic. Successful research programs often have a striking start, a first paper that is the best-known piece, but one rarely sees a rich orphan, an influential article that the author never followed up. My idealistic side wishes that quality would shine through, but the modern social sciences are too loud and crowded. Publishing a series of papers brings attention to your work through sheer mass: People are more likely to notice your ideas if they appear in several journals across several years. Beyond mere mass, a series of papers tells your readers that you're committed to your ideas, that you think they're important and worth years of your time. Some researchers hop capriciously from topic to topic, resulting in a vita with a quirky gallimaufry of publications. As a reader, I wonder why I should study an idea when its parent doesn't find it important enough to study more than once. And finally, a series of papers can reveal an idea's fecundity. By showing implications and extensions, moderators and boundaries, you show your readers what can be done with your idea, thus sparking their inspiration.

When thinking of research ideas, then, we should think expansively and plan ahead. The narrowest mind-set, and a common one among beginners, is simply trying to think of a study that could get published somewhere. As we argued in Chapter 1, strategic writers plan their research and think of it in terms of papers targeted to specific audiences and journals. Here we suggest thinking even more generally—instead of planning a lone paper, plan a series of studies, a network of linked papers that extend and elaborate your ideas. We're not trying to plan out our next 17 manuscripts—any number greater than one will suffice.

Trying to stretch your initial idea into a long program might take you farther than you thought, inspiring several new ideas for related papers—shockingly, creativity research has shown that deliberately trying to come up with creative ideas works (e.g., Christensen, Guilford, & Wilson, 1957). Or you might get the awkward experience of starting to talk but then finding yourself at a loss for words—some ideas are one-paper ideas, not cornerstones for a program. Either way, you've learned something essential: Your idea was more fertile or more barren than you thought. If you can think of a solid series, that's usually a sign that the idea is big enough to attract attention; if you can't, the idea might still be worth your time, but you can make a more realistic appraisal of whether it is worth the effort.

## WAYS TO BUILD IMPACT

### Be Discerning

Our lives are too hectic and brief to study every hypothesis that blithely wanders into our minds and trips over the extension cord duct taped to the carpet. Our bodies of work will have a bigger impact if we are discerning about our ideas. By committing only to our better ideas, we develop a better body of work and use our research time wisely. I write down most every idea I have, no matter how fringe, and they get placed into different mental piles.

- The first is the "must do" pile, the ideas I think are my best and connect directly to the problems I care most about. These are research ideas that are closest to my heart and that I think will be placed in the strongest journals. This pile gets written down in a document shared among the lab, so everyone can see and revise my ideas.
- The second is the "probably do" pile, the ideas that I'd like to do but lack the urgency or importance of the first pile. Often these are extensions or elaborations of "must do" ideas.
- The third is the "if time permits" pile, the ideas that seem neat but can't compete for time. These usually only come to fruition if collaborators or students get excited about them and want to take the lead.
- The fourth pile is the "compost pile," ideas that appeal to some fiendish or irrational streak of mine but are surely not worth studying. The main value of this pile is highlighting that not every idea is worth doing.

Beyond being discerning about our ideas for research, we should be discerning about what we seek to publish. Not all of our "must do" ideas pan out well:

File cabinets and flash drives are full of studies that ended badly, awkwardly, or mysteriously. People who seek mere publication will try to publish anything anywhere, and this is foolhardy. For one, the most insidious cost in life is opportunity cost. We can only do so much, so committing time to one project requires us to forsake others. And studies that don't end cleanly are usually hard to get published. As a result, a good paper takes less time and effort than a weak one, which will get kicked from journal to journal, undergoing extensive changes along the way, all for little gain in knowledge and impact. Efficiency alone suggests that we should euthanize our sickly projects rather than send them into the wild, where they'll be mauled by predators and ignored by potential mates.

What are signs that something shouldn't be published at all? Here are a few: the methods have severe flaws; the results lack a take-home message; the findings seem unlikely to replicate; and the message feels tortured, often because the data were collected for another purpose and don't dovetail with the new argument. The alternative is to try to "put a good face" on the data, to try to conceal the project's weaknesses and hope reviewers won't notice. I can assure you that they always notice. But even if they don't, a crueler fate awaits when readers notice, and the writer will diminish in their esteem. Remember that the only face on your work is your own.

Good writers should take pride in what they withhold—someone who publishes everything has no standards. As the culinary dictum goes, "Don't let your mistakes leave the kitchen."

## Write Review Articles

Once you have a small program of research in print, you should think about synthesizing it into a review article. Review papers get freakish attention. Anyone getting started in a field, planning readings for a grad seminar, or developing lectures about an unfamiliar topic will turn first to review papers. This has always been true, but it is probably becoming more so: There's too much primary literature to keep up with, so readers need the distilled version.

The phrase *review article* is inapt because the goal isn't to merely review what others have done. Like empirical articles, review articles must make a point. The best reviews advocate for a position, review the literature on both sides, address nuances that aren't easily worked into an empirical paper, and point to where the literature should go. Baumeister and Leary (1997) provided some excellent advice on writing review articles. Some of their reviews have been cited thousands of times, so they know of what they speak.

If they have written any, most researchers will find that their review articles are their most cited works. I'm thus always surprised at how few people consider writing review articles. One reason is surely the scope of the task: A long review article can be herculean. Another, I suspect, is that people have already said most of what they would want to say in edited book chapters, which eat up as much time as review articles but have less impact.

When planning a new area of research, you can use a hypothetical review article as a heuristic for coming up with ideas for the research program. If you were to write a review article, what kinds of studies would need to be done? What problems would need to be tackled, and with what methods? What new ideas should be infused into the literature? Think about it, do those studies, and then write the review article.

## Collaborate

Collaborating expands the range of things you can do and plugs you into a network of productive peers. Chapter 3 had much to say about collaboration—including a caution about choosing collaborators wisely that bears repeating—so here we'll simply reinforce the many virtues of working together with your peers. Strong teams can pool time, resources, and expertise, so they can execute projects that are hard for one person. Over the years, you'll find that working with other experts provides a constructive sense of humility, a discerning appraisal of what you do well and what others do better. And finally, one of the collaborators, if the team is big enough, will probably bring bagels.

## Organize a Community

Most areas of research are small areas—no problem is too technical or obscure to evade the keen eye of science. Even when the audience is big, the papers are usually generated by a ragtag band of merry researchers. By organizing this band into activities and institutions that attract attention and promote the group's work, you can promote your own work. Some obvious examples include proposing a special issue for a journal or sessions at conferences. In some cases you can make it easier for people to share their work, such as by creating an email list or social-media page that serves the dual goals of connecting interested researchers and allowing them to waste time on the Internet in the guise of science. And if you have time on your hands and a knack for administrative tasks—two facts you must never let your dean know—you can organize a preconference, a free-standing conference, or even a new scholarly society devoted to your area of research.

**Encourage Disagreement**

Once your papers get out there, you'll start to see them cited and discussed in other papers. The first times you see your work cited are eerie—it finally sinks in that people do read these papers and that we can't change what we committed to print. And eventually you'll see unflattering portrayals of your work. It might be gentle, such as pointing out a minor limitation or oversight, but it might be ghastly, such as mocking everything but your running head.

Disagreement is good. Your critics, be they gentle or ghastly, often have the most interest in your research:

They're the ones who are following your program, reading your papers, and conducting research inspired by it. Our pettier natures are tempted to thwart our critics, but you should encourage them. They don't bite, although they might nibble. These people will be good colleagues and collaborators.

## Seek External Funding for Your Research

When you have research grants, it's hard to answer a self-evident question like "Why should I seek external funding?" It's like asking cat owners why they like cats—you have to have one to really get it. Viewed pragmatically, grant writing gets done for three reasons. First, people write grants to avoid penury and homelessness. If you have a soft-money job or work in a department that requires external funding for tenure, you know what I mean. Getting grants is less about scientific pride and more about preventing the kids from wearing burlap clothes. If you plan to go into such a job after grad school, don't give away your ramen noodle stash to your office mates when you graduate. Second, people write grants to fund a good idea. For obvious reasons—employing staff, paying participants, and buying equipment—some research won't happen without external funding. Getting a grant thus lets you do research that is expansive and exciting. And finally, people write grants to develop their ideas for a research program. This shouldn't be the main reason for writing a grant proposal, but it's a nice consolation prize if the proposal isn't funded. Consistent with the writing-to-learn approach (Zinsser, 1988), writing about 3 to 5 years' worth of research is a great way to find out how good your ideas really are.

You should seek external funding, even if your department doesn't require it. Grant writing connects you into a broader world, allows you to execute bigger kinds of research, and can be weirdly gratifying even when the proposals go unfunded. I'm not snobbish about amounts and mechanisms and sponsors. There are only two kinds of grants: Those you get and those you don't. A $450 grant from a small foundation that lets you buy some necessary equipment gets you farther than a $450,000 proposal that a federal agency declined.

## WRITING TO AVOID

We never have enough time to write, so we need to be selective. Here are some kinds of writing worth avoiding.

### Chapters for Edited Books

In a quirky and compelling case study, Dorothy Bishop (2012) analyzed the citations of her publications. She sorted her papers into three categories: edited book chapters, empirical papers in journals, and conceptual and review articles in journals. Her conclusion? "Quite simply, if you write a chapter for an edited book, you might as well write the paper and then bury it in a hole in the ground." The journal articles—empirical or conceptual—dwarfed the book chapters, which had attracted few citations. This pattern is true for my work—some of my book chapters are buried deep enough to require spelunking equipment—and, I suspect, true for nearly everyone who works in a field that privileges traditional peer-reviewed journals over books, conference proceedings, and open-access outlets.

Why do book chapters get buried? One can consider many reasons, but I think Bishop (2012) nailed it:

> Accessibility is the problem. However good your chapter is, if readers don't have access to the book, they won't find it. In the past, there was at least a faint hope that they may happen upon the book in a library, but these days, most of us don't bother with any articles that we can't download from the Internet.

Journal articles are easily accessed online from anywhere in the world. Some publishers have placed some edited books into online databases, but reading the typical book chapter still requires a trip across campus to the library, where physical books sit crammed together like dogs in an animal shelter, each hoping for a short stint outside.

On the basis of impact alone, then, we should choose our invitations to contribute chapters wisely. But chapters have some other strikes against them. In most of the social, educational, and health sciences, book chapters count for less than articles when one's beans are counted. Book chapters also have deadlines, those banes of busy professors everywhere, and the deadlines are always when time is tight and enthusiasm is low. Many readers view chapters as dumping grounds for orphaned data and rewarmed ideas—not unfairly, I think—and thus expect to find little of value. Finally, chapters tend to be far longer than a typical manuscript, so their impact payoff is poor relative to the time spent writing them.

Given this bleak view of book chapters, why write them at all? Exhibit 10.1 shows some guidelines for when a chapter might be worth writing. If a chapter is about your own work, it will be easier, faster, and more interesting to write, and you can speculate and integrate in ways that are intellectually gratifying for you and your seven readers. If you're pretenure and the project looks interesting, go ahead and write the chapter. It connects you to other researchers and shows that your work is attracting attention. But if time is tight and you have better things to write, think thrice. I decline most of the invitations I receive. A simple

EXHIBIT 10.1. Some Reasons for Writing a Book Chapter

- The book seems prestigious, and it would be nice to be a part of the project.
- The editor is a friend or someone to whom you owe a favor.
- The chapter is a writing opportunity for your graduate students, who can take the lead under your mentorship (also known as "You guys write that and get back to me").
- You have a lot of time for writing and a thin backlog, so the chapter isn't crowding out more important projects.
- The chapter is about your research and ideas, which you know well.
- It pays a surprising amount of money.

e-mail that thanks the editor for thinking of you but notes that your writing backlog is too deep to take on another project will suffice. Either way, always accept or decline quickly so the editors can keep moving on their own project.

## Encyclopedias, Book Reviews, and Ephemera

The more seasoned among us remember a time when interested people would adopt a curious visage, walk to a shelf, and look something up in an encyclopedia or dictionary. Those books were a great way to avoid feeling left out when people were abuzz about the hottest trends in science and technology, like watches powered by small batteries instead of mainsprings, and they had a good run. Publishers still publish encyclopedias and dictionaries focused on professional topics, and they need experts to write entries. Libraries still buy these volumes, ensuring wide availability if not a wide readership. I suspect that all but a few of these books fall off the face of the earth. It's a shame—these books are great, and we would like our students to look things up using legitimate texts with entries composed by experts, not from the Internet, the home of ignorance in all caps—but it is what it is. There's no great harm in writing a short entry for a dictionary or encyclopedia, apart from more anxiety from your ever-looming backlog of more important projects, so use your time well.

Book reviews are another quirky kind of publication. I enjoy writing them—they force me to read and reflect about a book I'd like to read—but they reach a limited audience. The author is always in that audience, even if your review appears in a regional newsletter printed with a purple ditto machine, so think twice before ridiculing the book if you hate it. Book reviews also take surprisingly long to do, so don't do one unless you'd really like to read the book.

Our final category is ephemeral writing, the catchall for publications that aren't archived or cataloged: your blog, if you have one; guest posts for someone else's blog; and essays for newsletters, ranging from humble department house organs to periodicals that reach thousands of peers in a professional society. Such publications aren't peer reviewed, unless you count the flamboyant histrionics in a blog's comments section as a kind of review and your peers are rogues and desperados, but they can reach surprisingly large audiences. Some of my best writing is in this category, and I suspect that more people have read my guest blog posts and newsletter essays than most of my journal articles. Nevertheless, ephemeral writing, like anything usually requiring the Internet, can be a tremendous time sink. Blogging in particular can be an insidious form of procrastination—writing something fun and ostensibly productive to avoid writing something important—so don't neglect your journal articles.

## How to Write It All

If you're freaking out, wondering how you'll ever write all that stuff when the paper you just finished was so hard, freak not. You can do it. Most people have bad habits and mind-sets that hold them back, like believing that they need to wait for big blocks of time, inspiration, a feeling of readiness, a whole day at home, an uncluttered desk, and other fictions that let us procrastinate with a clean conscience. A bit of behavior change and a solid routine are usually enough to get a lot of papers written.

Motivational aspects of productive writing are a book unto themselves. One of those books is *How to Write a Lot* (Silvia, 2007), but there are many more that address time management, procrastination, and good habits (e.g., Boice, 1990; Goodson, 2013; Lambert, 2013). My perspective is that we have much less control over our time than we think. Most of us believe, against all reason and experience, that there's time in the week to be found for writing. But, of course, our time is quickly set upon by the usual brigands: teaching, service, fires to put out and start, and bushels upon bushels of e-mail.

If the workweek is largely a maelstrom of chaos, then I think it is fruitless to adopt intricate time-management systems or to set temporal goals farther out than 1 week. I have seen people set 6 or 8 weeks' worth of goals for their paper—"I'll spend two weeks on the Intro, one on the Method, two on the Results . . . "—but such plans usually come to grief, dashed on the shoals of grading, web browsing, and providing vital service on the Associate Vice Provost for Parking's Utilization Committee.

We should accept that much is out of our hands and then control what we can—our own behavior. We can choose a time for writing, sit down and write during that time, and then stop when that time is over. Scheduling writing is how people who publish a lot write a lot. Making a writing schedule guarantees time to write and shelters your writing from the inanity and chaos of the workweek. And after a couple weeks, writing at that place at that time becomes a sturdy habit, and writing is no longer something you choose, hope, or want to do—it's just another habitual reflex, like brushing your teeth, winding your watch, and grousing about the kids these days.

Try it—start with 4 to 6 hours a week for writing. Four hours is enough to write most of what you'd like to write and more than most people spend writing. You'll be surprised how much you get written.

## WRAPPING EVERYTHING UP

As professors, teachers, and mentors, we know all too well that giving people fish feeds them only for a day. But teaching them to fish—ideally with PowerPoint slides, short essay tests, and discursive lectures on history and theory—feeds them for a semester, after which they sell their ichthyology textbook back. This book, with its combination of trust-me-on-this and here's-why, has tried to give and to teach. Life is too short, and the publication process too long, to learn the hard way—it's easier to learn from other people's mistakes, especially when they are embarrassing and hilarious. But most of writing's many decisions require people to develop their own informed perspective, so some things you'll learn only from practice and rejection.

This book developed a few themes: We should write for impact and influence, not merely for publication; we should respect the opportunity cost of writing and be selective in what we pursue; we should view writing as a craft, a skill to honor, not as a mere step in the research process; we should be reflective and plan for writing's many decisions, ranging from picking journals to selecting references; and we should sweat the small stuff until it breaks down and confesses.

Psychologists are a hardened lot—it comes from dealing with students who say, "I majored in psych because all my friends say I'm a good listener" yet don't listen when told the assigned readings—so this journey through the netherworld of academic writing and publishing will end with a taciturn goodbye, a flinty nod instead of sassy kisses on both cheeks. These chapters distilled most of what I've seen and heard from my years in the peer-reviewed trenches. Now you should get to writing and dig some trenches of your own—pack a big thermos and give me a flinty nod if our trenches should cross.

# References

Adair, J. G., & Vohra, N. (2003). The explosion of knowledge, references, and citations: Psychology's unique response to a crisis. *American Psychologist, 58*, 15–23. doi:10.1037/0003-066X.58.1.15

American Psychological Association. (2010). *Publication manual of the American Psychological Association* (6th ed.). Washington, DC: Author.

Arkin, R. M. (Ed.). (2011). *Most underappreciated: 50 prominent social psychologists describe their most unloved work.* New York, NY: Oxford University Press.

Atkinson, J. W. (1964). *An introduction to motivation.* New York, NY: Van Nostrand.

Baker, S. (1969). *The practical stylist* (2nd ed.). New York, NY: Thomas Y. Crowell.

Bartneck, C., & Kokkelmans, S. (2011). Detecting *h*-index manipulation through self-citation analysis. *Scientometrics, 87*, 85–98. doi:10.1007/s11192-010-0306-5

Batson, C. D. (1975). Rational processing or rationalization? The effect of disconfirming information on a stated religious belief. *Journal of Personality and Social Psychology, 32*, 176–184. doi:10.1037/h0076771

Batson, D. (2011). Bet you didn't know I did a dissonance study. In R. M. Arkin (Ed.), *Most underappreciated:*

*50 prominent social psychologists describe their most unloved work* (pp. 208–212). New York, NY: Oxford University Press.

Baumeister, R. F., & Leary, M. R. (1997). Writing narrative literature reviews. *Review of General Psychology, 1*, 311–320. doi:10.1037/1089-2680.1.3.311

Beall, J. (2012). Predatory publishers are corrupting open access. *Nature, 489*, 179. doi:10.1038/489179a

Bem, D. J. (2011). Feeling the future: Experimental evidence for anomalous retroactive influences on cognition and affect. *Journal of Personality and Social Psychology, 100*, 407–425. doi:10.1037/a0021524

Bennett, C. M., Baird, A. A., Miller, M. B., & Wolford, G. L. (2010). Neural correlates of interspecies perspective taking in the post-mortem Atlantic salmon: An argument for proper multiple comparisons correction. *Journal of Serendipitous and Unexpected Results, 1*, 1–5.

Benton, D., & Burgess, N. (2009). The effect of the consumption of water on the memory and attention of children. *Appetite, 53*, 143–146. doi:10.1016/j.appet.2009.05.006

Berlyne, D. E. (1960). *Conflict, arousal, and curiosity.* New York, NY: McGraw-Hill. doi:10.1037/11164-000

Bhattacharjee, Y. (2013, April 26). The mind of a con man. *The New York Times Sunday Magazine*, p. MM44.

Bishop, D. (2012, August 29). *How to bury your academic writing.* Retrieved from http://blogs.lse.ac.uk/impactof socialsciences/2012/08/29/how-to-bury-your-academic-writing/

Bohannon, J. (2013). Who's afraid of peer review? *Science, 342*, 60–65. doi:10.1126/science.342.6154.60

Boice, R. (1990). *Professors as writers.* Stillwater, OK: New Forums.

Brehm, J. W., & Cole, A. H. (1966). Effect of a favor which reduces freedom. *Journal of Personality and Social Psychology, 3*, 420–426. doi:10.1037/h0023034

Bridwell, N. (1966). *Clifford takes a trip*. New York, NY: Scholastic.

Brown, C. (1983). Topic continuity in written English narrative. In T. Givón (Ed.), *Topic continuity in discourse* (pp. 313–341). Amsterdam, the Netherlands: John Benjamins. doi:10.1075/tsl.3.07bro

Brysbaert, M., & Smyth, S. (2011). Self-enhancement in psychological research: The self-citation bias. *Psychologica Belgica, 51*, 129–137. doi:10.5334/pb-51-2-129

Carey, B. (2011, November 3). Fraud case seen as a red flag for psychology research. *The New York Times*, p. A3. Retrieved from http://www.nytimes.com

Chen, I., Wu, F., & Lin, C. (2012). Characteristic color use in different film genres. *Empirical Studies of the Arts, 30*, 39–57.

Chenoweth, E., & Stephan, M. J. (2011). *Why civil resistance works: The strategic logic of nonviolent conflict.* New York, NY: Columbia University Press.

Christensen, P. R., Guilford, J. P., & Wilson, R. C. (1957). Relations of creative responses to working time and instructions. *Journal of Experimental Psychology, 53*, 82–88. doi:10.1037/h0045461

Cooper, H. (2010). *Reporting research in psychology: How to meet journal article reporting standards.* Washington, DC: American Psychological Association.

Cooper, J. (2011). What's in a title? How a decent idea may have gone bad. In R. M. Arkin (Ed.), *Most underappreciated: 50 prominent social psychologists describe their most unloved work* (pp. 177–180). New York, NY: Oxford University Press.

Cooper, J., & Jones, E. E. (1969). Opinion divergence as a strategy to avoid being miscast. *Journal of Personality and Social Psychology, 13*, 23–30. doi:10.1037/h0027987

de Carle, D. (1979). *Complicated watches and their repair.* New York, NY: Bonanza Books.

Dempsey, P. (2008). *Small gas engine repair* (3rd ed.). New York, NY: McGraw Hill.

DeWall, C. N., Lambert, N. M., Slotter, E. B., Pond, R. R., Deckman, T., Finkel, E. J., . . . Fincham, F. D. (2011). So far away from one's partner, yet so close to romantic alternatives: Avoidant attachment, interest in alternatives, and infidelity. *Journal of Personality and Social Psychology, 101,* 1302–1316. doi:10.1037/a0025497

Doros, G., & Geier, A. B. (2005). Probability of replication revisited: Comment on "An alternative to null-hypothesis significance tests." *Psychological Science, 16,* 1005–1006. doi:10.1111/j.1467-9280.2005.01651.x

Dunkel, H. B. (1969). *Herbart and education.* New York, NY: Random House.

Dunlosky, J., & Ariel, R. (2011). The influence of agenda-based and habitual processes on item selection during study. *Journal of Experimental Psychology: Learning, Memory, and Cognition, 37,* 899–912. doi:10.1037/a0023064

Eggers, D. (2000). *A heartbreaking work of staggering genius.* New York, NY: Simon & Schuster.

Eidelman, S., Crandall, C. S., & Pattershall, J. (2009). The existence bias. *Journal of Personality and Social Psychology, 97,* 765–775. doi:10.1037/a0017058

Few, S. C. (2012). *Show me the numbers: Designing tables and graphs to enlighten* (2nd ed.). Burlingame, CA: Analytics Press.

Fine, M. A., & Kurdek, L. A. (1993). Reflections on determining authorship credit and authorship order on faculty–student collaborations. *American Psychologist, 48,* 1141–1147. doi:10.1037/0003-066X.48.11.1141

Fowler, J. H., & Aksnes, D. W. (2007). Does self-citation pay? *Scientometrics, 72,* 427–437. doi:10.1007/s11192-007-1777-2

Franchak, J. M., & Adolph, K. E. (2012). What infants know and what they do: Perceiving possibilities for walking through openings. *Developmental Psychology, 48*, 1254–1261. doi:10.1037/a0027530

Garner, B. A. (2009). *Garner's modern American usage* (3rd ed.). New York, NY: Oxford University Press.

Gibbs, R. W., Jr. (1994). *The poetics of mind: Figurative thought, language, and understanding.* New York, NY: Cambridge University Press.

Givón, T. (1983). Topic continuity in spoken English. In T. Givón (Ed.), *Topic continuity in discourse* (pp. 343–364). Amsterdam, the Netherlands: John Benjamins. doi:10.1075/tsl.3.08giv

Glazek, K. (2012). Visual and motor processing in visual artists: Implications for cognitive and neural mechanisms. *Psychology of Aesthetics, Creativity, and the Arts, 6*, 155–167. doi:10.1037/a0025184

Goodson, P. (2013). *Becoming an academic writer: 50 exercises for paced, productive, and powerful writing.* Los Angeles, CA: Sage.

Greenblatt, S. (2011). *The swerve: How the world became modern.* New York, NY: Norton.

Greengross, G., Martin, R. A., & Miller, G. (2012). Personality traits, intelligence, humor styles, and humor production ability of professional stand-up comedians compared to college students. *Psychology of Aesthetics, Creativity, and the Arts, 6*, 74–82. doi:10.1037/a0025774

Gruber, H. E. (1989). The evolving systems approach to creative work. In D. B. Wallace & H. E. Gruber (Eds.), *Creative people at work: Twelve cognitive case studies* (pp. 3–24). New York, NY: Oxford University Press.

Hamelman, J. (2004). *Bread: A baker's book of techniques and recipes.* Hoboken, NJ: Wiley.

Hamilton, D. P. (1990). Publishing by—and for?—the numbers. *Science, 250*, 1331–1332. doi:10.1126/science.2255902

Hamilton, D. P. (1991). Research papers: Who's uncited now? *Science, 251*, 25. doi:10.1126/science.1986409

Hoggard, L. S., Byrd, C. M., & Sellers, R. M. (2012). Comparison of African American college students' coping with racially and nonracially stressful events. *Cultural Diversity & Ethnic Minority Psychology*, *18*, 329–339. doi:10.1037/a0029437

Hyland, K. (2001). Humble servants of the discipline? Self-mention in research articles. *English for Specific Purposes*, *20*, 207–226. doi:10.1016/S0889-4906(00)00012-0

Inbar, Y., Cone, J., & Gilovich, T. (2010). People's intuitions about intuitive insight and intuitive choice. *Journal of Personality and Social Psychology*, *99*, 232–247. doi:10.1037/a0020215

Iverson, G. J., Lee, M. D., Zhang, S., & Wagenmakers, E. (2009). $p_{rep}$: An agony in five Fits. *Journal of Mathematical Psychology*, *53*, 195–202. doi:10.1016/j.jmp.2008.09.004

Johnson, D. J., & Rusbult, C. E. (1989). Resisting temptation: Devaluation of alternative partners as a means of maintaining commitment in close relationships. *Journal of Personality and Social Psychology*, *57*, 967–980. doi:10.1037/0022-3514.57.6.967

Kaufman, S. B., DeYoung, C. G., Gray, J. R., Jiménez, L., Brown, J., & Mackintosh, N. (2010). Implicit learning as an ability. *Cognition*, *116*, 321–340. doi:10.1016/j.cognition.2010.05.011

Kelly, G. A. (1955). *The psychology of personal constructs: Vol. 1. A theory of personality.* New York, NY: Norton.

Kerr, N. L. (1998). HARKing: Hypothesizing after the results are known. *Personality and Social Psychology Review*, *2*, 196–217. doi:10.1207/s15327957pspr0203_4

Killeen, P. R. (2005). An alternative to null-hypothesis significance tests. *Psychological Science*, *16*, 345–353. doi:10.1111/j.0956-7976.2005.01538.x

Ladinig, O., & Schellenberg, E. G. (2012). Liking unfamiliar music: Effects of felt emotion and individual differences. *Psychology of Aesthetics, Creativity, and the Arts*, 6, 146–154.

Lakoff, G., & Johnson, M. (1980). *Metaphors we live by*. Chicago, IL: University of Chicago Press.

Lambert, N. M. (2013). *Publish and prosper: A strategy guide for students and researchers*. New York, NY: Routledge.

Lamiell, J. T. (1981). Toward an idiothetic theory of personality. *American Psychologist*, 36, 276–289. doi:10.1037/0003-066X.36.3.276

Lamiell, J. T. (1987). *The psychology of personality: An epistemological inquiry*. New York, NY: Columbia University Press.

Ledgerwood, A., & Sherman, J. W. (2012). Short, sweet, and problematic? The rise of the short report in psychological science. *Perspectives on Psychological Science*, 7, 60–66. doi:10.1177/1745691611427304

Mayer, M. (1983). *I was so mad*. Racine, WI: Western.

McCarthy, M. A. (2012). Toward a more equitable model of authorship. In R. E. Landrum & M. A. McCarthy (Eds.), *Teaching ethically: Challenges and opportunities* (pp. 181–190). Washington, DC: American Psychological Association. doi:10.1037/13496-016

Murayama, K., Pekrun, R., & Fiedler, K. (2014). Research practices that can prevent an inflation of false positive rates. *Personality and Social Psychology Review*, 18, 107–118. doi:10.1177/1088868313496330

Nicol, A. A. M., & Pexman, P. M. (2010a). *Displaying your findings: A practical guide for creating figures, posters, and presentations*. Washington, DC: American Psychological Association.

Nicol, A. A. M., & Pexman, P. M. (2010b). *Presenting your findings: A practical guide for creating tables*. Washington, DC: American Psychological Association.

Nusbaum, E. C., & Silvia, P. J. (2011). Are intelligence and creativity really so different? Fluid intelligence, executive processes, and strategy use in divergent thinking. *Intelligence, 39,* 36–45. doi:10.1016/j.intell.2010.11.002

Oh, S.-Y. (2005). English zero anaphora as an interactional resource. *Research on Language and Social Interaction, 38,* 267–302. doi:10.1207/s15327973rlsi3803_3

Oh, S.-Y. (2006). English zero anaphora as an interactional resource II. *Discourse Studies, 8,* 817–846. doi:10.1177/1461445606067332

Peirsman, Y., & Geeraerts, D. (2006). Metonymy as a prototypical category. *Cognitive Linguistics, 17,* 269–316. doi:10.1515/COG.2006.007

Pinker, S. (1999). *Words and rules: The ingredients of language.* New York, NY: Basic Books.

Quirk, R., Greenbaum, S., Leech, G., & Svartvik, J. (1985). *A comprehensive grammar of the English language.* New York, NY: Longman.

Reis, H. T., & Stiller, J. (1992). Publication trends in *JPSP*: A three-decade review. *Personality and Social Psychology Bulletin, 18,* 465–472. doi:10.1177/0146167292184011

Ring, K. (1967). Experimental social psychology: Some sober questions about some frivolous values. *Journal of Experimental Social Psychology, 3,* 113–123. doi:10.1016/0022-1031(67)90016-9

Risen, J. L., & Gilovich, T. (2008). Why people are reluctant to tempt fate. *Journal of Personality and Social Psychology, 95,* 293–307. doi:10.1037/0022-3514.95.2.293

Rotella, K. N., Richeson, J. A., Chiao, J. Y., & Bean, M. G. (2013). Blinding trust: The effect of perceived group victimhood on intergroup trust. *Personality and Social Psychology Bulletin, 39,* 115–127. doi:10.1177/0146167212466114

Sagan, C. (1995). *The demon-haunted world: Science as a candle in the dark.* New York, NY: Random House.

Salovey, P. (2000). Results that get results: Telling a good story. In R. J. Sternberg (Ed.), *Guide to publishing in psychology journals* (pp. 121–132). Cambridge, England: Cambridge University Press. doi:10.1017/CBO9780511 807862.009

Sawyer, R. K. (2011). *Explaining creativity: The science of human innovation* (2nd ed.). New York, NY: Oxford University Press.

Schimmack, U. (2012). The ironic effect of significant results on the credibility of multiple-study articles. *Psychological Methods, 17,* 551–566. doi:10.1037/a0029487

Schulz, K. F., Altman, D. G., Moher, D., & the CONSORT Group. (2010). CONSORT 2010 statement: Updated guidelines for reporting parallel group randomized trials. *Trials, 11*(32). Available at http://www.trialsjournal.com/content/11/1/32

Schwartz, C. A. (1997). The rise and fall of uncitedness. *College & Research Libraries, 58,* 19–29.

Scott, L. (2004). Correlates of coping with perceived discriminatory experiences among African American adolescents. *Journal of Adolescence, 27,* 123–137. doi:10.1016/j.adolescence.2003.11.005

Silvia, P. J. (2001). Nothing or the opposite: Intersecting terror management and objective self-awareness. *European Journal of Personality, 15,* 73–82. doi:10.1002/per.399

Silvia, P. J. (2002). Self-awareness and emotional intensity. *Cognition and Emotion, 16,* 195–216. doi:10.1080/02699930143000310

Silvia, P. J. (2003). Self-efficacy and interest: Experimental studies of optimal incompetence. *Journal of Vocational Behavior, 62,* 237–249. doi:10.1016/S0001-8791(02)00013-1

Silvia, P. J. (2005). What is interesting? Exploring the appraisal structure of interest. *Emotion, 5,* 89–102. doi:10.1037/1528-3542.5.1.89

Silvia, P. J. (2006). *Exploring the psychology of interest.* New York, NY: Oxford University Press. doi:10.1093/acprof:oso/9780195158557.001.0001

Silvia, P. J. (2007). *How to write a lot: A practical guide to productive academic writing*. Washington, DC: American Psychological Association.

Silvia, P. J. (2010). Confusion and interest: The role of knowledge emotions in aesthetic experience. *Psychology of Aesthetics, Creativity, and the Arts, 4,* 75–80. doi:10.1037/a0017081

Silvia, P. J. (2012). Mirrors, masks, and motivation: Implicit and explicit self-focused attention influence effort-related cardiovascular reactivity. *Biological Psychology, 90,* 192–201. doi:10.1016/j.biopsycho.2012.03.017

Silvia, P. J., & Brown, E. M. (2007). Anger, disgust, and the negative aesthetic emotions: Expanding an appraisal model of aesthetic experience. *Psychology of Aesthetics, Creativity, and the Arts, 1,* 100–106. doi:10.1037/1931-3896.1.2.100

Silvia, P. J., & Gendolla, G. H. E. (2001). On introspection and self-perception: Does self-focused attention enable accurate self-knowledge? *Review of General Psychology, 5,* 241–269. doi:10.1037/1089-2680.5.3.241

Silvia, P. J., & Nusbaum, E. C. (2011). On personality and piloerection: Individual differences in aesthetic chills and other unusual aesthetic experiences. *Psychology of Aesthetics, Creativity, and the Arts, 5,* 208–214.

Silvia, P. J., Nusbaum, E. C., Berg, C., Martin, C., & O'Connor, A. (2009). Openness to experience, plasticity, and creativity: Exploring lower-order, higher-order, and interactive effects. *Journal of Research in Personality, 43,* 1087–1090. doi:10.1016/j.jrp.2009.04.015

Silvia, P. J., & Phillips, A. G. (2004). Self-awareness, self-evaluation, and creativity. *Personality and Social Psychology Bulletin, 30,* 1009–1017. doi:10.1177/0146167204264073

Silvia, P. J., Winterstein, B. P., Willse, J. T., Barona, C. M., Cram, J. T., Hess, K. I., . . . Richard, C. A. (2008). Assessing creativity with divergent thinking tasks: Exploring the reliability and validity of new subjective scoring methods. *Psychology of Aesthetics, Creativity, and the Arts, 2*, 68–85. doi:10.1037/1931-3896.2.2.68

Simmons, J. P., Nelson, L. D., & Simonsohn, U. (2011). False-positive psychology: Undisclosed flexibility in data collection and analysis allows presenting anything as significant. *Psychological Science, 22*, 1359–1366. doi:10.1177/0956797611417632

Simmons, J. P., Nelson, L. D., & Simonsohn, U. (2012). A 21 word solution. *Dialogue: The Official Newsletter of the Society for Personality and Social Psychology, 26*(2), 4–12.

Soler, V. (2007). Writing titles in science: An exploratory study. *English for Specific Purposes, 26*, 90–102. doi:10.1016/j.esp.2006.08.001

Steinbeck, J. (1962). *Travels with Charley: In search of America*. New York, NY: Viking.

Sternberg, R. J. (Ed.). (2000). *Guide to publishing in psychology journals*. Cambridge, England: Cambridge University Press. doi:10.1017/CBO9780511807862

Stevens, C. D., & Ash, R. A. (2001). The conscientiousness of students in subject pools: Implications for "laboratory" research. *Journal of Research in Personality, 35*, 91–97. doi:10.1006/jrpe.2000.2310

Swann, W. B., Jr., Hixon, J. G., Stein-Seroussi, A., & Gilbert, D. T. (1990). The fleeting gleam of praise: Cognitive processes underlying behavioral reactions to self-relevant feedback. *Journal of Personality and Social Psychology, 59*, 17–26. doi:10.1037/0022-3514.59.1.17

Sword, H. (2012). *Stylish academic writing*. New York, NY: Oxford University Press.

Tobias, R. B. (2012). *Twenty master plots: And how to build them*. Cincinnati, OH: Writer's Digest Books.

Trafimow, D., MacDonald, J. A., Rice, S., & Clason, D. L. (2010). How often is $p_{rep}$ close to the true replication probability? *Psychological Methods, 15*, 300–307. doi:10. 1037/a0018533

Turner, S. A., Jr., & Silvia, P. J. (2006). Must interesting things be pleasant? A test of competing appraisal structures. *Emotion, 6*, 670–674. doi:10.1037/1528-3542. 6.4.670

U.S. Department of Health and Human Services. (2012, November 26). *Guidance regarding methods for de-identification of protected health information in accordance with the Health Insurance Portability and Accountability Act (HIPAA) privacy rule*. Washington, DC: Author. Retrieved from http://www.hhs.gov/ocr/privacy/hipaa/ understanding/coveredentities/De-identification/guid ance.html

Vines, T. H., Albert, A. Y. K., Andrew, R. L., Débarre, F., Bock, D. G., Franklin, M. T., . . . Rennison, D. J. (2014). The availability of research data declines rapidly with article age. *Current Biology, 24*, 94–97. doi:10.1016/j. cub.2013.11.014

Wendig, C. (2011). *250 things you should know about writing* [Kindle edition]. Available at http://terribleminds.com/ ramble/chucks-books/250-things-about-writing/

Wicherts, J. M., & Bakker, M. (2012). Publish (your data) or (let the data) perish! Why not publish your data too? *Intelligence, 40*, 73–76. doi:10.1016/j.intell.2012.01.004

Wicherts, J. M., Borsboom, D., Kats, J., & Molenaar, D. (2006). The poor availability of psychological research data for reanalysis. *American Psychologist, 61*, 726–728. doi:10.1037/0003-066X.61.7.726

Witt, E. A., Donnellan, M. B., & Orlando, M. J. (2011). Timing and selection effects within a psychology subject pool: Personality and sex matter. *Personality and Individual Differences, 50*, 355–359. doi:10.1016/j.paid.2010. 10.019

Wolfe, T. (1975). *The painted word*. New York, NY: Farrar, Straus and Giroux.

Zabelina, D. L., Felps, D., & Blanton, H. (2013). The motivational influence of self-guides on creative pursuits. *Psychology of Aesthetics, Creativity, and the Arts, 7*, 112–118. doi:10.1037/a0030464

Zinsser, W. (1988). *Writing to learn*. New York, NY: Quill.

Zinsser, W. (2006). *On writing well: The classic guide to writing nonfiction* (30th anniversary edition). New York, NY: HarperCollins.

# Index

# About the Author

**Paul J. Silvia, PhD,** is an associate professor of psychology at the University of North Carolina at Greensboro. His books include *How to Write a Lot: A Practical Guide to Productive Academic Writing* (2007) and *Exploring the Psychology of Interest* (2006). His research has been supported by several grants from the National Institutes of Health, and he received the Berlyne Award, an early career award given by APA Division 10 (Society for the Psychology of Aesthetics, Creativity, and the Arts) for his research on interest and curiosity.